Reflections on Lancaster

Terry Potter

Wilmslow, England

Copyright ©, Terry Potter, 1992

All Rights Reserved

No part of this publication may be reproduced, stored in a retrieval system, or transmitted in any form or by any means – electronic, mechanical, photocopying, recording, or otherwise – without prior written permission from the publisher.

First published in 1992 by Sigma Leisure – an imprint of Sigma Press, 1 South Oak Lane, Wilmslow, Cheshire, SK9 6AR, England.

Whilst every effort has been made to ensure that the information given in this book is correct, neither the publisher nor the author accept any responsibility for any inaccuracy.

British Library Cataloguing in Publication Data

A CIP record for this book is available from the British Library.

ISBN: 1-85058-309-9

Cover design by

Martin Mills

Typesetting and graphics by

Sigma Press

Printed and bound by: Manchester Free Press

Preface

Lancaster – the name resonates with the history of Lancashire. But despite being a city of history, with its mediaeval Castle atop the hill dominating all, modern Lancaster is of another Lancashire, a Lancashire that few outside the region realise exists. This is the Lancashire that is not reeling from the demise of mills and the textile industry, a Lancashire that is not of cobbled streets, back alleys and mean thoroughfares.

The city was at one time beholden to its industries, with their workforces of thousands, often at the mercy of powerful families who, had they not been of a largely benevolent nature, could well have been the 'Grabgrinds' of their day. Nearly all of those old industries have disappeared, for Lancaster has changed. The sites of huge old factories are now used for housing, and modern industrial and commercial estates.

A great deal of old Lancaster has gone, been demolished, consigned to the dustbin of history – and a very good thing too. That seemingly endless supply of books of old photographs illustrating the quaintness of life in the days of our grandparents, with outside privies and communal water pumps, tightbuilt terraced housing with yards, and the roads only occasionally busy with horse-drawn vehicles, rarely admits how those houses were often dark and insanitary and damp, the people hungry and out of work. Life for many was almost unrelieved drudgery and struggle – a bathroom, a regular job and a balanced, nutritious diet being the stuff of dreams.

It was not all bad, of course, and Lancaster, despite having its share of hard times, was fortunate in that the handful of industrialists who controlled its economic well-being had social consciences, and the pages of the city's history are littered with references to their benevolent philanthropy. Lancaster became an individualistic town (it achieved city status only as recently as 1937), one that today savours its past while not being afraid to dispense with it, if occasion demands. It has kept many of the best of its old buildings, but has some outstanding new ones, such as the Government Department offices at Mitre Yard, below the Castle, and indeed the Sainsbury's on Cable Street.

Lancaster has continued unabated its long literary, artistic and academic traditions, of major importance being the growth of the University of Lancaster since the 1960s, and makes good use of its libraries and museums, its canal and old industrial buildings and redundant churches.

This book is not a history of Lancaster. The shelves of local libraries groan under the weight of tomes describing every nook and cranny. It delves only a little back to Roman times and does not march methodically and chronologically up to the present day. Nor is it a walker's book, telling the reader to turn left here, right there, take this or that path, consult map and compass.

What this book does do is explore aspects of the city and reflect on what has taken place and what is taking place. It takes more note of people than dates and buildings, for though the city is of buildings, and its history of dates, the atmosphere of Lancaster derives from the people who have lived and worked here over hundreds of years, from the high and mighty Lord Ashton, to the humble artisan.

The value of local newspapers for investigating the history of towns is inestimable, much information coming from the advertisements, as well as the editorial columns. A main source for 'Reflections on Lancaster' has been the files of three newspapers, the Lancaster Guardian (founded 1837), the Morecambe Visitor (1874) and the long-deceased Lancaster Gazette. Use has also been made of various issues of the old Lancaster Observer. As for pictures, these have been acquired over many years, many coming from readers of newspapers on which the writer has been employed. Thanks go to them and to all others who have, sometimes unwittingly, provided information which has now been distilled into 'Reflections on Lancaster.'

Terry Potter

Contents

Bones, Romans and Commerce — 1

A look at Lancaster's colourful characters, mainly from yesteryear. A brief history and an explanation of why Lancaster looks the way it does today.

The Man who fell out of love with Lancaster — 11

All about Lord Ashton and the in-fighting that caused him to renounce his association with the city. A tour of the Ashton landmarks.

Industrial Giants — 22

We all know of Storeys and Waring and Gillow, but how did they come to be in Lancaster? Read about Lancaster's railways and canal, and how it once had a thriving shipping industry

Churches and Churchmen — 31

Catholic or C of E, Lancaster has its share of denominations, churches and chapels. And even a chapel that is now a theatre.

Horses, The Sands and World War II — 39

Today's traffic may be bad, but imagine having to dodge between the horses. Walking across the sands has always been a local adventure, even in wartime. But were they really the good old days?

The White Lund Explosion   49

Lancaster's most famous disaster could have been much worse, and there have been many other near-misses.

'Lancaster Worthies'   55

Lancaster genius knows no bounds – from music to motor cars, and from art to commerce. There have been famous medical men, and even the inventor of the plastic eye.

Politics and Politicians   69

Politics and corruption sometimes go hand-in-hand, and this has occasionally been the case in Lancaster. Early Socialist struggles, Suffragettes and hard-fought elections all feature strongly.

Crime and Policemen   75

Some gory and infamous cases loomlarge in Lancaster, with the prison conveniently to hand. Masterly detective work, draconian laws and tales of sorrow feature in this chapter.

A City and its Landmarks   85

City Status achieved in 1937. Regal links as the Duchy of Lancaster. Pomp and pageantry, concluding with a tour of the city's landmarks.

1

Bones, Romans and Commerce

Bricks and Bones

Lancaster is an old city and every so often shows it by throwing up mysteries of the past. Human bones have often been found, from old burial grounds and battles. Once, the skeleton of a tall figure, probably that of a man, *'in a reasonable state of preservation'*, was unearthed during demolition of old buildings near Phoenix Street. Who was he? We shall never know.

On another occasion, a skull and other bones were dug up by roadworkers, outside the Castle. These were probably those of felons who had been hanged and their bodies buried *'within the precincts of the prison'*.

But Lancaster dates to much more ancient times, and it seems that just about every time major building work takes place, evidence of the Romans comes to light.

Much important archaeological work took place in the 1950s, when excavations were carried out round the Priory and Parish Church.

Exploration has continued at every opportunity since, including exposing the Bath-house, which is now something of a tourist attraction.

Roman Forts

Much of what we know dates from the 1950s, when for the first time it was possible to examine an extensive area of remains and learn more of the layout and chronological sequence of successive forts on the hilltop now dominated by the Castle.

When a major dig was started at the start of the decade, there were revelations of military buildings of the second and third centuries AD. These extended Northwards to the Lune beyond the line of the Wery Wall, the massive Northern defence wall of the fourth century fort.

The third century fort, whose garrison was the *Ala Sebusiana*, a cavalry regiment 500 strong, had substantial buildings constructed on foundations of river cobbles set in blue clay.

As 'digs' progressed, the main building of this period was identified as the Commandant's house. This was a large rectangular building with ranges of rooms along each side of a central stone-flagged courtyard, 46 ft. x 60 ft. The walls were solidly built to a width of two and a half feet.

The Romans were not averse to the comforts of life – especially in the chilly climate of Britain – and the stokehole for the central heating system was found at the rear of the building. Here a fire fed hot air through a brick-lined aperture in the outer wall and circulated it under the hollow floors of the rooms.

A second-building was identified as a granary, and beyond these third century remains were the foundation trenches of timber-framed buildings belonging to two successive forts of the second century AD.

River Lune

Many theories have been propounded over the years of what Lancaster was like in Roman times and even about where the River Lune flowed during distant centuries.

When redevelopment was taking place around the Library in Market Square in the late 1950s, Roman pottery was unearthed from a bed of sand. The Samian ornamental pottery had not been made in England but brought by the Romans when they occupied this country.

One local historian, the late T. Pape, whose works are well worth searching out and who became an authority on Northern England, held the view that the tons of fine sand excavated in the Market Square area showed that this area had once been part of the bed of the Lune.

The Lune probably flowed over Green Ayre, Cheapside, Lower Church Street and Market Square and under what is now Littlewoods, to King Street.

Pape believed that long before the Romans, the Lune was turned by the hill on which Lancaster Castle stands in a South Westerly direction. This left the great outcrop North, and not South, of the river.

Records from as recently as four centuries ago show Green Ayre low lying, unbuilt upon and surrounded by a mill race which flowed where Parliament Street, North Road and Damside Street are now situated.

Digging up the Past

The investigation of the past is a continuous process and every opportunity is taken to literally dig it up. Lancaster is fortunate that the City Council has shown a positive attitude when these opportunities have presented themselves, and that there has been an archaeological department at the University to provide the knowledge and expertise required.

Much important work was carried out as recently as 1990, when excavations took place at a site near the bus station in Damside. These tried to trace the former course of the Lune, get some idea of what the lie of the land had been, and perhaps even track down where the Romans had harboured their ships.

Among several discoveries was a large early Roman wall. There were also mediaeval remains, unusual for Lancaster, for most of the 'old' buildings in the city, (with the exception of places such as the Priory and Parish Church and the Castle), date from Georgian times. Fires and the digging of foundations for more modern buildings have obliterated the evidence of previous centuries.

That there are few really old buildings in the city makes early accounts of Lancaster of more than ordinary interest.

About 1700, Celia Fiennes, who traversed much of England by horse, wrote:

> *'The situation of Lancaster is very good. The church neatly built of stone; the castle, which is just by; both on a very great ascent from the rest of the town, and so is in open view; the town and river lying round beneath Lancaster town is old and much decayed. In the river are great weirs of falls of water made for salmon fishing, where they hand their nets and catch great quantities of fish, which is near the bridge. The town seems to be not much in trade as some others, but the great store of fish makes them live plentifully as also the great plenty of all provisions. The streets are some of them well pitched and of good size. I cannot say the town seems a lazy town, and there are trades of all sorts.'*

Past People of Lancaster

And what of the people who lived here?

Let's look at Augustine Greenwood, a merchant and wholesale dealer during the reigns of the later Stuart monarchs. Augustine was son and heir of a prosperous Lancaster merchant, John Greenwood, who lived in Market Street and was one of the leading Presbyterians of Lancaster.

In 1687, while his father was Mayor, Augustine married as his second wife a widow, Alice Townson. She was a daughter of Thomas North, of Docker, and had previously been married to Christopher Hopkin, of Holme House, near Kirkby Lonsdale, and Thomas Townson, a Kirkby Lonsdale grocer.

A neighbour of the Greenwoods was William Stout, devout Quaker, ironmonger, grocer, tobacconist and part ship-owner. He wrote of the event which made Alice a widow for the third time in April 1701. Greenwood died suddenly in Market Street.

According to Stout,

> 'He fell down dead in the Market Street, a little above the town hall, to the great astonishment of people in the street.'

Stout noted that Alice's first husband had died very suddenly also, and that her second was drowned in the Lune while trying to save someone's life. Such was life and death in 17th and 18th century Lancaster for a merchant of the town.

The Fraudulent Mayor

Life could be pretty chaotic when even the people who were supposed to be in charge could not be trusted.

In 1680, the Mayor, Thomas Corless, was thrown out of office forever. This was for a series of offences, including being drunk at fairs, the Assizes 'and other public and private times' and for having pocketed money meant to have been sent to the Castle for the welfare of prisoners.

The Nineteenth Century

An impression of the state of the town in the early years of the 19th century can be gleaned from the pages of the Lancaster Gazette. In 1809, it carried an advertisement showing that all was not well.

> 'Notice is hereby given, That a Meeting of the Inhabitants of the Borough and Town of Lancaster, will be held at the Town Hall, in Lancaster, on Wednesday, the 17th May, 1809, at eleven o'clock in the forenoon, for the purpose of taking into consideration the present Bad State of Repair of several of the New Streets in Lancaster, which have been lately laid open, and are now used as public streets through the town; and also to fix on some plan of getting the same repaired and supported in future.'

What was churning up the streets? The stage coaches, perhaps. At this time, the King's Arms and Royal Oak Inns were leading staging inns in Lancaster, with coaches, including the Royal Mail, leaving for Liverpool, Kendal, Penrith and Carlisle, Ulverston and Whitehaven, Glasgow, Edinburgh, Newcastle, Port Patrick and all parts of Scotland.

Floggings and Tough Times

Life was pretty tough for most people, and justice tended to be of the physical kind. Floggings were the order of the day for even quite trivial offences. Thus, in 1871, according to the Lancaster Observer,

> *'Joseph Betterson, a lad, was charged on remand with stealing 12 pocket knives, the property of John Booth, Stone Well. Betterson admitted his guilt and was ordered to receive 20 strokes from a birch.'*

But you had to be tough in those days to survive even the sanitary conditions. At a meeting in the same year of the charmingly named Sanitary and Slaughter House Committee, it was proposed, during a discussion about making four abattoirs into one,

> *'that the garbage and everything else should never be thrown upon the ground, as hitherto, but that it should be deposited in cisterns, and taken away at once, so that no filth would be allowed to accumulate and cause a nuisance!'*

The Mayor considered it a matter of urgency.

> *'Now the hot weather was coming on, they ought to do what they could to free the place from the filthy nuisance in the centre of the town ... which was endangering the health of the inhabitants.'*

With life being for many, little more than a matter of mere survival, the attraction of emigrating to the United States and Canada was strong.

Newspapers, local and national, were full of advertisements by agencies willing to provide information and advice, and 'guaranteeing' employment for mechanics, clerks, drapers, agriculturists and others.

Just how many took advantage of emigration we shall probably never know, but it is certain that it was many. It is also certain that travelling on the ships was a pretty sickening business for those of little means.

They travelled steerage, down among the cargo and bilges, packed like sardines and breathing the atmosphere created by hundreds of unwashed, perspiring human bodies.

Demolition

Much of what could be described as 'Old Time' Lancaster fell to the demolition gangs of the 1950s. One example, pictured, was St. Mary's Place, tucked away off St. Mary's Gate, under the walls of the Castle.

Here there was an old water pump over a well in the corner of a yard. Although on demolition in 1956, it had been disused for many years, the photograph on the facing page, taken in 1927 by Samuel Thompson, (a well-known Lancaster photographer), shows the pump in good working condition, and nearby a housewife drawing water from a communal tap.

Plenty of Pubs

Many areas of Lancaster were changed almost beyond recognition in the 1950s and 1960s, including the demise of many old pubs.

One of these premises was on the site adjoining the Judges' Lodgings, at the foot of St. Mary's Gate. At one time, it had been the Mitre Inn, but by the time it was demolished in 1959 it had been a confectionery shop of many years' standing; the houses of many of its customers were swept away at around the same period.

The Mitre was only one of many inns that were formerly in this neighbourhood, when China Street was the narrower China Lane. At the Market Street junction of old China Lane stood the Feathers Hotel.

In the short distance between there and the modern Black Bull, (which stands on the site of a former hostelry of that name), were the Castle Hotel, the Volunteer, the Spink Bull and the Hole in the Wall.

Pubs were a way of life. There were virtually no licensing restrictions, and little imagination is needed to appreciate the mayhem that broke out when rough, tough workingmen decided to settle their differences.

Another street that boasted a surfeit of pubs and hotels was Lower Penny Street, between Horse Shoe Corner and the junction with Brock Street and Common Garden Street. Among them were the Queen's Hotel, the Bear and Staff, the Wheatsheaf and the Fleece Hotel.

Bashful Alley

Lancaster has saved a number of the weinds and ginnels that formerly made up much of the town. These include 'Bashful Alley', cutting from Market Street to King Street, and the name of which has exercised local historians for years.

There are at least two stories of the name's derivation. One is that sailors courted their girlfriends there. The other is that when the Post Office was in Market Street, young men congregated at the corner of King Street and Market

Reflections on Lancaster

Street. Bashful young ladies would then use the alley to escape their unwelcome attentions.

Colourful Characters

Is life less colourful these days? Every generation seems to think so, but it is undeniable that right up to the Second World War there were individuals whose eccentricities were, to put it kindly, 'pronounced'.

Two in Lancaster were particularly memorable. Lending considerable colour to life up to the 1930s was 'Neddy' Pennington, a diminutive figure who appeared regularly at the auction marts

Samuel Thompson's photograph of St. Mary's Place, 1927

and markets in both Lancaster and Garstang, and the other was 'Cumberland Joe'.

Neddy

'Neddy' was a sprightly little man with a luxuriant growth of moustache. He carried a wicker basket filled with filbert nuts and doled them out to customers with a half-pint glass. With bowler-hat, ill-fitting raincoat and natty little apron, he was not averse to giving the public a burst of dancing to whip up trade.

Cumberland Joe

'Cumberland Joe' spoke in broad dialect of that county at considerable volume. He was an odd-jobbing gardener, and by all accounts a good one.

However, he had an abiding fixation in life: the merits of 'Cumberland eggs and bacon.' On seeing a person of lesser girth, he would roar, *'Call 'em legs. What you want is some good Cummerland eggs and bacon inside yer.'* This accompanied with withering looks at the unfortunate adult or child by now cowering in acute embarrassment.

Demise of Smith's and the Co-op

Smith's

Old characters have gone, and so too have many of the old businesses of the city, businesses that Lancastrians of the day thought would last for ever. One particularly well-remembered enterprise was T. D. Smith's, grocers and provisions merchants, with a large block of property in Penny Street, Frances Passage and Mary Street.

The business had been founded in 1858, in a single shop at No. 15 Penny Street by young grocer Thomas Davidson Smith and, like Topsy, it 'growed and growed'.

Only four years later, Smith took over larger premises in Frances Passage. The period between the First and Second World Wars saw great growth, premises being bought in Grange in 1925, and other outlets being opened at Settle and Arnside. It was a progressive firm. About 1950, it started a profit-sharing scheme, and in the mid-1950s a non-contributory pension scheme.

The old Lancaster Co-op

However, in 1960, F. Brian Smith, head of the firm, had to announce the sale of the premises in Lancaster. Although a successor firm did take over, the real story of T. D. Smith's was over.

The Co-op

And who would have thought that the old Lancaster Co-op, part of the commercial fabric of the city, would close its premises in the very heart of Lancaster. The 'Co-op', a way of life, had its origins in 1860, when a group of working people held a meeting.

These years were not good times for Lancaster. The population of about 14,000 was dwindling, working people were worried and discontented, with the highest-paid artisans getting only about 25s (£1.25) a week.

From 1860 to the late 1980s, the Co-op grew to cover three counties. It absorbed other societies, opened new shops and offices, expanded, the huge premises on the corner of Church Street and New Street being the hub of the mighty empire. Life without the old Lancaster Co-op just isn't the same.

2

The Man who fell out of love with Lancaster

James Williamson II

It would be less than surprising if the ghost of Lord Ashton, a great Lancaster industrialist, walked the streets of the city. If it does, it is probably an unhappy ghost.

In October 1936, the estate of the Rt. Hon. James Williamson, first Baron Ashton, D.L., J.P., of Ashton Hall and Ryelands, Lancaster, who had died in 1930, leaving what was thought to be £9,500,000, was re-sworn because it was found that the amount should have been £10,501,595.

Extraordinarily, this man left no will. Half his property went to his widow and half to his daughter, Countess Peel. On the previous valuation of £9,500,000, death duties were reported to have amounted to £4,750,000.

Ashton's image

Lord Ashton in the public memory has conflicting roles. Some view him as a mercenary opportunist, a man who would spy on his workers to identify slackers and shirkers and agitators, others as a benevolent dictator who went out of his way to be good to Lancaster and his workers, who many a time paid a man suffering illness or accident.

The truth no doubt lies somewhere in between, but there is one certainty. Lord Ashton hated the idea of trade unionism in his great factories, and it was the result of trade unionists' and Socialists' activities that he rejected the town of his birth.

When he took over his father's floor-coverings business, it was already reasonably prosperous. He extended it enormously though, opening new factories at home and abroad. At one time, Lord Ashton employed 3,500 people in Lancaster alone.

In the political arena

A friend of Gladstone, Lord Ashton, born in Lancaster's Church Street in 1842, became Liberal MP for the Lancaster Division in 1886. He gave up the seat in 1895, and was created Lord Ashton in the same year.

He married three times and had two daughters but no son. The third Lady Ashton was awarded the C.B.E. at the beginning of 1937, for political and public services in Lancashire. She became a much-loved figure in the Lancaster area, particularly for her work for children's and animals' charities.

There are few stories of Lancaster as problematical as the curious love-hate relationship of Lord Ashton and the city.

Dominating the skyline is the massive baroque Ashton Memorial, and in Dalton Square, the grand Town Hall and huge statue of Queen Victoria – all given to Lancaster by Lord Ashton. Down on New Quay, beyond St. George's Quay, are still remnants of the huge complex of Lune Mills, the vast Linoleum works.

It was with the manufacture of that ubiquitous product that Lord Ashton gathered in his immense fortune.

The Problems Begin

For years the relationship with Lancaster was pleasant. The City Council fawned at Lord Ashton's feet, understandably, in that he was a powerful employer, and Lord Ashton was far from backward in his benevolence to Lancaster.

But the latter years of the 19th century and the early years of the 20th were

Lord Ashton, from a portrait at Lancaster Town Hall

troubled, tough times for many. Midway through June 1909, the unemployed of Lancaster petitioned the Board of Guardians for more work to be found. They claimed if nothing was done, '*2,100 men, women and children will have to go to the Union*' (Workhouse).

In the same year, Lord Ashton married for the third time. It should have been a happy year for him, but there is evidence that this is the year in which he fell out of love with Lancaster. His bride was Mrs. Whalley, of Lancaster, daughter of the late Rev. R. Daniel, Vicar of Oswaldwick, near York.

By this time, Lord Ashton had been a widower for nearly five years. His second wife, who had been Miss Jessie Henrietta Stewart, daughter of James Stewart, of Clapham, had died in Octo-

Lancaster Town Hall, given by Lord Aston

ber 1904, after 24 years of wedded life. (His first wife, the daughter of Joseph Gatey, of Keswick, died in 1877.)

Until 1909, Lord Ashton's career had glittered. His father James had been Mayor of Lancaster in 1864 and 1865, and although James II never filled that position, he served on the Council for Castle Ward, and represented the Lancaster Division in Parliament in the Liberal interest from 1886 to 1895, after which he was raised to the peerage. He was High Sheriff of the County in 1885, and a Deputy Lieutenant, as well as a magistrate for Lancaster Borough and County, and the County of London.

Ashton Hall

When he was raised to the peerage by Lord Rosebery, he took the title Baron Ashton. This came from Ashton Hall, a mansion on the Southern outskirts of Lancaster, which he bought from Col. J.P.C. Starkie in 1884.

Today Ashton Hall is the home of Lancaster Golf Club – surely one of the most magnificent golf clubhouses in the country.

The Letters

However, some tarnish had accrued. There was much talk in 1895 that he 'bought' his title. That mini-scandal blew over, but the major storm came in 1909. Here, he ran into trouble with the local branch of the ILP, and things rapidly deteriorated.

The tone of a letter written by Lord Ashton in November 1909, just about summed up the situation:

> *'For many years past, strangers have been brought to the town, and have addressed meetings in such language as could not possibly be defended by right-minded people, and have made false statements, knowing them to be false ... These outsiders have held their meetings as near as possible to my house – Ryelands – indulging in most insolent language, and going so far as to describe me as a thief and a robber.'*

In 1910, following some particularly 'dirty' electioneering by opponents, Lord Ashton really let loose, penning one of the most vitriolic letters in the area's history.

> *'Only on one occasion during the whole of my life have I taken the slightest notice of the lying and slanderous attacks which have been made upon me during Parliamentary elections, made even though I was not the candidate, by those who knew their statements to be absolutely false ...*
>
> *'In consequence of my political opinions I*

have been singled out as the object of a succession of malicious attacks by the Conservative Party of this Division. They use every endeavour to make the constituency believe that whatever I have contributed to the happiness and welfare of those amongst whom I live has been done with a political motive; in other words, that it has been done solely with the object of influencing the votes of the electors ...

'In fact, ever since the Parliamentary election of 1886, everything that I have done to brighten the lives of those who needed help in Lancaster and the neighbourhood, without reference to polities, religious persuasion, or any other test whatever, to promote the interests of charitable and other institutions in the district, or to lighten the burdens of the ratepayers – in fact, everything I have done to benefit my fellow men, has stirred up the malice of my political opponents, and they have shown their hatred by circulating abusive and lying rumours against myself at Parliamentary elections.

'I may as well say that over and over again surprise has been expressed that I should continue in the face of such treatment to trouble myself any further about the affairs of Lancaster, but hitherto I have always steadily refused to be influenced by the conduct of my slanderers to depart from my usual course.

'I have now, however, made up my mind that if this sort of thing is to continue, I shall not take any further interest in Lancaster or the neighbourhood, and thus save myself from a repetition of those disgusting exhibitions of political rancour, as well as from an expenditure of many thousands a year.'

By 1911, the worm had turned. Following the cancellation of a wage rise to his employees, it was then all downhill. Lord Ashton dropped out of public life altogether, as far as Lancaster was concerned, becoming a recluse.

His relationship with Lancaster is aptly illustrated by a letter he wrote to the Mayor in August 1912, following an invitation to be present at a visit of the King.

'My wife and I deeply regret that we can not be with you on the occasion of the King's visit on the 24th inst., as we have ceased to take any interest in the affairs of Lancaster.'

Withdrawal of Support

At the start of 1912, he had already made clear the way things were to be. On his 69th birthday, he departed from his custom of 30 years of providing a birthday party to about 300 Skertonians. No invitations were extended. Other charities were also suspended, much to the disappointment of many old and poor townspeople.

Later he made a decision that affected the local hospital and about a thousand Lancaster children. He resigned from his office as trustee and vice-president of the Royal Lancaster Infirmary, an institution to the cost of which he had subscribed at least £10,000.

In addition, the Jubilee Town Mission, with four branches and a thousand children as members, would be wound up. Lancaster reeled from the blows. What had they done?

In October 1912, Lord Ashton wrote a letter to his employees after granting a wage rise.

> 'I have to acknowledge the receipt of the resolutions passed at your meetings on the 21st inst., for which I very sincerely thank you. I am also deeply gratified by the references made in the Sympathetic speeches in support of those resolutions to the wilful and deliberate misrepresentations of myself by those whom you rightly describe as the "lower type" of those who differ from me politically – misrepresentations which have been pursued with incredible malignity for the last 25 years ...
>
> 'Surely consideration of the welfare of the town, saying nothing of what was due to one who has lived here all his life and arrived at the age of close on 70, and who, for more than 40 years, has endeavoured to contribute in some measure to the happiness and welfare of his fellows, ought to have saved him from such expressions of rancour – even political rancour – to which he has so long been subjected. But this, it would seem, is not to be, for since my letter to the constituency in January, 1910, this evil work is still being pursued therefore I cannot but feel that the case is absolutely hopeless.
>
> 'Anyhow, there is something left; the loyalty and goodwill of my own people – and that is what I now value most. The interests of the town and neighbourhood, therefore, I must leave in the hands of those whose purity of motive, as I said on a recent occasion, is beyond question. My only regret is that this was not done years ago. I refrain from saying more at present'.

The following year, Lancaster property owners petitioned Lord Ashton to build a new weaving shed at his huge factory.

Although agreeing to the proposal, he made very clear, that *'he deeply resents and has great cause to be terribly grieved at the malicious and cruel way in which his motives in what he has done for the town have been misconstrued.'*

St. Annes benefits

By and large, Lord Ashton transferred his affections and philanthropy to St. Annes. The beautiful Ashton Gardens there are just one of his principal benefactions. £10,000 was given for the War Memorial in the Ashton Gardens, £10,000 for the endowment of the hospital, a further £5,000 for the hospital building fund, and £20,000 in connection with the purchase of the Tramways.

The first Freedom of the Borough of St. Annes was conferred upon him, the presentation taking place at Ryelands in February 1923, *'in the simplest manner and a total absence of ceremony.'*

It is open to conjecture as to how much of this would have come Lancaster's way, had Lord Ashton's political opponents been a little less strident.

Lady Ashton

Lord Ashton thus cut his ties with Lancaster. This left him in the curious situation of living out his days, taking no notice of a town in which everywhere there were reminders of his previous philanthropy.

He died at Ryelands House on May 27, 1930, disappointed and disillusioned. Lady Ashton went on to become one of the most popular figures in the North West. When Lord Ashton withdrew from local public life, she had more or less followed his example. Apart from devoting herself to 'good causes' during the First World War, she was but little seen by the people of Lancaster and district.

But after his death, she plunged into public work, becoming a veritable 'Lady Bountiful', taking a particular interest in the welfare of children and animals, and the unemployed in the district.

There was genuine regret at her death in July 1944, and in her will she left a series of bequests to RSPCA branches, many philanthropic societies, churches and the unemployed.

Landmarks of Ashton

Ashton Memorial

Lord Ashton's greatest building in Lancaster is the Ashton Memorial in Williamson Park, conspicuous for many miles. Hundreds of thousands of people see it every year from the M6.

Reflections on Lancaster

In 1962, a huge amount of damage was caused when the great copper dome suffered when the wooden framework underneath caught fire. Firemen from all over North Lancashire fought the blaze, which had started when workmen were renovating the dome.

Renovation

By 1986, the condition of the Memorial had become so bad that something had to be done. It had been boarded off as a no-go area for several years – pieces of masonry having developed the unfortunate habit of falling off – and the whole structure was restored to its former glory.

It was a big job. A team of scaffolders had to erect 50,000 feet of tubing using 10,000 scaffold fittings and 4,000 walkboards before they reached the top of the massive dome.

The Memorial opened in May of the following year. It was an immediate success as a major tourist venue, with a multi-screen 'Edwardians' exhibition telling the story of the life and times of Lord Ashton. A Butterfly House was also there, in the old Palm House next to the memorial.

The Design and Designer

Lancastrians have irreverently called the

Opposite: The Ashton Memorial pictured during renovation in the 1980s. Locally known as 'The Structure' or even as 'The Jelly Mould'

Ashton Memorial the 'Jelly Mould'. James Belcher, President of the Institute of British Architects, was the designer, and building started in 1905. The Morecambe newspaper, The Visitor, commented:

> *'The new erection will be a symmetrical building of an ornamental character, in the Classic style of architecture. It will be built in white Portland stone, and when completed will stand some 150 feet above the level of the bold promontory selected as the site. The whole of the stonework will be dressed in Lancaster.'*

Belcher was already a famous architect and the Ashton Memorial brought him further fame and fortune. In 1907, he was recommended to the King as the recipient of the Royal Gold Medal annually conferred on

> *'some distinguished architect or man of science or letters who had designed a building of high merit, or produced a work tending to promote or facilitate the knowledge of architecture, or the various branches of science connected therewith.'*

(They believed in long sentences in those days!).

In Memory of Who?

Just what is the Ashton Memorial, built at the enormous cost of £87,000, a memorial to? One story is that it was originally to be to Lord Ashton's first wife, Alice. However, after re-marrying twice, he diplomatically changed it to be a memorial to 'deceased members' of his family.

The Queen Victoria Statue

The Queen Victoria statue in Dalton Square, facing another of Lord Ashton's gifts, the Town Hall, is also very impressive. Below an enormous plinth supporting the bronze of Victoria, are four mighty lions and then friezes of outstanding figures from industry, art and science.

We find Derby, the great 19th century politician, rubbing shoulders with Aberdeen, Prime Minister during the Crimean War; two more Home Secretaries, Russell and Peel, the latter famous for founding the police; Salisbury, three times Prime Minister; Beaconsfield, better known as Benjamin Disraeli; and Gladstone, who came unstuck over Home Rule, for Ireland. Also jostling for recognition are other Prime Ministers: Palmerston; Rosebery, one of whose contributions to history was being first chairman of London County Council; and Melbourne, the man who guided the young Queen Victoria when she came to the throne.

Look out for Bright, born the son of a

cotton spinner near Rochdale. He rose to become Chancellor of the Duchy of Lancaster and was deeply involved in Irish problems and the Anti-Corn Laws League; and Frankland, the eminent chemist born at Churchtown. They are with such figures as Turner the painter, and Lister, the founder of modern antiseptic surgery.

Note Owen, the Socialist reformer who at least brought some humanitarianism to the Industrial Revolution; Macaulay, the historian; Darwin the evolutionist; Dickens, who made at least two visits to Lancaster; Stephenson, of 'Rocket' fame; Irving, the actor; Tennyson, the Poet Laureate; Pitman, of Shorthand; Florence Nightingale; Hill, the originator of the Penny Post; and Whewell, the Lancaster-born son of a joiner, who became a leading scientist, philosopher, theologian and astronomer. And if you look very closely, you will find one James Williamson, father of Lord Ashton.

The Queen Victoria statue, a gift of Lord Ashton, on Dalton Square

Reflections on Lancaster

One of the 'friezes' of famous men and women around the base of the Queen Victoria statue. Note James Williamson (extreme right), Lord Ashton's father.

3

Industrial Giants

Waring and Gillow

Until about 30 years ago, the Lancaster furniture-making company Waring and Gillow was known throughout the land and in many other parts of the world. It could trace its history to 1729, and was famed for its furnishings and fittings for many of the most famous stately mansions and ocean-going liners.

For instance, when the Queen Mary was being built in the mid-1930s, it was to Waring and Gillow that the contract went for the interior decoration and furniture. The Lancaster artist-craftsmen worked on rare and beautiful woods from Canada West Africa, French Guyana, Brazil and Scandinavia, as well as Britain.

Some idea of the quality of the firm's work is given in that they furnished and decorated the first-class restaurant, the most impressive of any ship built at that time. The staircase, (forward and aft), and all the accompanying entrances, the main hall, the library, the observation lounge, the grand corridors were all provided by Waring and Gillow.

These carried on the traditions of Chippendale, Sheraton and Hepplewhite, started by the firm's founder, Robert Gillow. The firm linked with the Liverpool company Waring in 1900.

In 1961, it all came to an end. One of the first victims of a trend of decline in the major industries of Lancaster, advertisements appeared in the local press the following year, giving notice of the proposed sale of the workshop of Waring and Gillow.

This was very substantial, covering about 8,000 square yards, the frontages stretching about 275 feet in North Road, and 365 feet in St. Leonardgate.

At the time of the closure, the firm was owned by Universal Stores and employed more than 300. The benefit of hindsight suggests that the demise of Waring and Gillow's workshops in Lancaster had much to do with the rise of relatively cheap air travel. The consequent collapse of the building of oceangoing liners left a great hole in the firm's business.

Lune Mills

Alongside the River Lune, beyond St. George's Quay, will be found what is left of an industrial complex that not so long ago was the largest of its kind in the world: the Lune Mills of the Lancaster magnate Lord Ashton.

Today, the Lune Mills area is scarcely even a shadow of its former self, many of the old buildings having been demolished or put to other uses.

The start of the business came in 1844, when Alderman James Williamson founded a new business in England. On frames 12 yards long and a yard and a half wide – dimensions which became standard the world over – the first English oilcloth was prepared by hand.

Williamson cornered the market and the business grew at a frantic rate to become the employer of many thousands. It seemed there was always a job available at James Williamson and Son Ltd.

Williamson died in 1879, handing on to his son, also called James, who was to become Lord Ashton. He soon revealed himself as a commercial genius, who took the products of Williamson's throughout the world. It was under his guidance that the company achieved its international standing.

In the early days, the products of the firm were oil baizes, which became known as Lancaster Cloth, and imitation leather cloths.

But it was in Lord Ashton's time that the most important commercial decision was taken, with the concentration on the manufacture of floorcloth, Linoleum and Lancaster Window Blind Cloth. Where would the British home, and indeed, the homes of the Western World, have been without the ubiquitous Lino?

But eventually, there were dozens of other products, some of them put to the most surprising of uses.

The products of Williamson's included fabrics for upholstery, pram covers and bags, curtains, washable wall coverings and shoe linings. The material for the peaks of gaolers' hats in China were made by Williamson's, as was the covering for children's toy carriages in Buenos Aires. Williamson's even helped the cinema industry, for at the vast works at Lancaster, silver-coated cloth for cinema screens was produced.

In September 1962, the directors recommended to shareholders a merger with Messrs. Michael Nairn and Greenwich Ltd., of Kirkaldy, the large, Scottish Linoleum company, and nearly 120 years of directly local tradition came to an end, nearly 120 years of keeping hearth and home together for thousands of Lancaster folk.

Storeys

Another of the great industries that has all but vanished was Storeys, who operated from White Cross Mills, opposite the Royal Lancaster Infirmary, and Moor Lane Mills in the city itself, and Low Mill in Caton village. The enterprise had its beginnings in 1849, and it went on to become one of the largest employers of local labour.

White Cross Mills, now the home of the local studio of Granada Television and a host of other concerns, has an almost 'Disneyesque' castle facade.

Storey's was founded by Thomas Storey, later Sir Thomas, and his brothers, Edward and William.

The company's original purpose was the manufacture of table baize, or American cloth. However, it later started making other types of leathercloth and coverings, and when the age of plastics arrived, became one of the leading makers of plastic sheeting. Many members of the public will remember it for 'Con-Tact', the handy sticky material that, at one time, seemed to line every kitchen drawer and cover every shelf.

But White Cross Mills closed in the 1980s, when the city was going through a particularly severe run of big factory closures, and there is little of the original Storeys empire left.

Another Storeys company, Joseph Storey and Co. Ltd., of the Heron Chemical Works, Moor Lane, founded in 1860, was bought out in 1959, severing local independence, and further demonstrating the decline of big employers like Storeys over the last quarter-century. This case is typical of the industrial problems Lancaster has had to surmount.

The same year had seen the announcement of the closure of the carding and spinning departments at Low Mill, Caton. The Caton mill had been bought by Storeys in 1864, at the same time as the Moor Lane mill. It was originally a corn mill until 1783, later being run by the Hodgsons, an old Caton family, and later still by the Greg family, who sold it to Storeys.

Most of the members of the Storey family took a prominent part in local public life, some living to ripe old ages. Edward, for example, was 84 when he died in 1913.

Apart from the business, he devoted his life to public service, being on Lancaster

Town Council for many years, the Board of Guardians, (of which he was vice-chairman), and taking great interest in the Royal Albert Hospital and the church. For half a century, he was also warden at Christ Church. By his will, he disinherited any children or grandchildren becoming Roman Catholics.

The Railways

In the hey-day of industrial Lancaster, much of the products of the huge factories of firms like Williamson's, Storeys and Gillow left the town by rail, and Lancaster was fortunate in being well served by railway from an early date.

The town's first railway, the Lancaster and Preston, obtained its Act in 1837, the line opening in June 1840. This more than halved the time it took to get to London, which formerly had taken a day. Later came the Lancaster and Carlisle line, opened in December 1846.

The Canals

The railways knocked on the head a form of transport which had been important to Lancaster – the canal.

Today, it is a major leisure facility, including the charming little 'branch' between Galgate and Glasson Dock. What was at the time described as the 'Northern Level' was opened in November 1797, with great ceremony. This stretched from Tewitfield in the North to Preston in the South, a distance of $41^1/_2$ miles, and was built without a single lock.

It is for chiefly this reason that it follows what can only be described as a circuitous course. Locks are found only on the 'branch' canal.

The day of opening was quite an occasion. The Canal Committee, *'accompanied with colours and music'*, made their way from their office to boats with representatives of all involved in building or using the canal, for a cruise on the new waterway. Instructions for the day were explicit. 'The Bee' and 'Ceres' were to be fitted up for the particular friends of the committee and the most respectable persons in Lancaster.

> *'A few guns to be planted on the rubbish heap on the Moor, a signal given to be fired at half-past nine. Music to be played ... and a salute of guns to be fired when the committee take the barge with another salute as the committee barge enters the Aqueduct!'*

The boats then turned and travelled to Galgate in the South, prior to returning to Lancaster. There the whole company, headed by bands and a detachment of Volunteers, marched in procession via

Old boats on the Lancaster Canal

Reflections on Lancaster

A bridge over the branch of the Lancaster Canal from Galgate to Glasson Dock

Penny Street, Church Street, Castle Hill and Market Street to the King's Arms, where in accordance with the tradition of those days, the affair ended with a grand banquet.

In 1802, the Canal Company advertised *'a pleasant voyage'* from Lancaster to Preston, for the famous Preston Guild celebrations by packet boat.

> *'For safety, economy and comfort, no other mode of conveyance could be so eligible as the packet boats; for there the timid might be at ease and the most delicate mind without fear.'*

The construction of the canal from Tewitfield to Kendal was completed in 1819, and a passenger service by packet boats drawn by horses was regularly started in 1820.

Shipping Industry

In its early days, Lancaster and its Port, Glasson Dock, was a busy shipbuilding and repairing centre. All along the quays were yards, where vessels were turned out regularly. Notices such as, *'On Thursday last, a fine new ship was launched from Messrs. Caleb Smith and Co.'s yard, near this town'*, were frequent. The ship-repairing tradition only petered out as recently as 1960, when the last yard at Glasson Dock, Nicholsons, closed.

Nicholsons closed their yard to concentrate on making silencers for motor vehicles, quite a change from when they made vessels which plied routes all round Britain and across the seas.

Although the last big ship to be built at Glasson was around the end of the 19th century, in 1926 the first Fleming lifeboat was built there, and just before the Second World War a big yacht was rebuilt. The firm was mostly occupied in the repair of trawlers, dredgers and yachts.

The Ryelands

One of the ships lived on for many years until it was destroyed by fire at Morecambe in 1970. The three-masted schooner built at Glasson in the 1880s as the 'Ryelands' became a tourist attraction at Morecambe berthed off the Stone Jetty.

The ship was used in the films 'Moby Dick' as the 'Pequod' and 'Treasure Island' as the 'Hispaniola', and in a television series, 'The Buccaneers', as the 'Delipa', and she was still registered under that last name when taken to Morecambe by Peter Latham, a partner with his father in the Arcadian Restaurant in the resort.

On the same day, and at the same time, as the 'Moby Dick' was destroyed by fire, Morecambe's Alhambra Theatre went up in flames.

Reflections on Lancaster

Glasson Dock, the port of Lancaster, formerly a ship-repairing and ship-building centre

Internment in the Wagon Works

One of the most unusual uses of old industrial premises in Lancaster came in the First World War. For many years, until the first decade of the 20th century, the Wagon Works in Caton Road were major employers, turning out trams and railway rolling stock for all over the world. They were more or less closed down in 1908.

However, in the First World War, they were brought into use for the internment of German 'Aliens', and later for the manufacture of torpedoes.

After the First World War, the works were again closed, and at the same time the National Projectile Factory in Caton Road, (see Chapter Six), closed. Two major blows to the Lancaster industrial scene in times when unemployment was already high.

The outbreak of the First World War in August 1914 presented the Government with a huge problem. They had to round up all 'unregistered aliens' in the country – of which there were many thousands and the problem was, where to put them?

In Lancaster, the Wagon Works provided an ideal solution, so the buildings were prepared for an expected influx of 2,000. A special Reserve Company of the Royal Welsh Fusiliers was also called in to act as guards.

The first batch of 'aliens' arrived in the last week of August 1914, from Liverpool, a train being run alongside and partly into the Works. A company of the Cheshire Regiment formed an armed guard for accompanying the 'aliens' on the train. Later, another batch arrived from Hull, and more groups arrived at intervals.

The prisoners were searched on arrival and medically examined. Everywhere there was barbed wire to make sure they did not escape. Daily rations were fixed by the War Office: Bread, one and a half pounds, or biscuits, one pound; meat, 8 oz, or preserved meat, half ration; fresh vegetables, 8 oz; butter or margarine, 1 oz; condensed milk, one twentieth of one 1 lb tin; tea, half oz, or coffee, one oz; sugar, two oz; salt, half oz.

Perhaps understandably, the area was consumed by rumour of what was happening at the Wagon Works and spy stories abounded. In truth, most of the people confined were perfectly honest, respectable folk who had the misfortune at that time to be of German origin. There was a good deal of jingoism fanned by thinly-disguised racism. It was not a very savoury interval in local history.

4

Churches and Churchmen

The Great Churches

Lancaster's history is steeped in the Church, much of it in the troubled and intolerant times of the 17th and 18th centuries. Of the 13 Martyrs associated with the Diocese of Lancaster, nine were executed in the city, and all were among 85 Martyrs from England, Wales and Scotland who were beatified by Pope John Paul II as recently as 1988. But it is not the purpose of this book to dwell on the distant past, but on more recent times.

The First Bishop

A new Suffragen See of Lancaster was created in 1936, its first Bishop being a man fondly remembered in the city, the Rev. Benjamin Pollard. At the time of his appointment, he was the Vicar of Lancaster, Canon of Blackburn Cathedral.

He became Bishop when only 46, a married man whose wife, prior to marriage, had been Marjorie Bradbury, member of an old Sheffield family of silversmiths.

Pollard gained both popularity and respect because he was a straight-talking, down-to-earth character who associated easily with the ordinary people.

He was educated at Manchester Grammar School and Manchester University, where he was a research student in chemistry, but later turned his attention to an ecclesiastical career. After being ordained priest, he was a curate at Weaste, and later a curate at Sheffield Cathedral and afterwards Presentor. Later he became Rector of Bradfield, Yorks, followed by a similar position as Rector of St. Chrysostom, Victoria Park, Manchester, and was for two years, chaplain at Manchester Infirmary.

The Priory and Parish Church

These occupy a particular place in the affections of Lancastrians. The church, the largest in the area, makes a fitting partner to the Castle, both being conspicuous on the city's skyline.

Rev. H. A. Bland

A particularly well-known Vicar here was the Rev. H. A. Bland, who had been Rector of Morecambe. Born in

Reflections on Lancaster

Lancaster's Priory and Parish Church

Streatham, he was educated at Giggleswick and Christ Church College, Cambridge, and trained at Cuddleston College, Oxford.

Bland was ordained in 1925, and certainly saw the other side of life. In 1929, he became Warden of Gonville and Caius College (Cambridge) Mission in the slum districts of Battersea.

Apart from a spell at Peterborough, where he became the first Vicar of St. Barnabas' in 1933, he came to Lancashire and stayed. He was Vicar of Clitheroe in 1942, Rural Dean of Whalley 1945 to 1950, Rector of Morecambe 1950 to 1955, before going to Lancaster.

Among many of his innovations, was the founding of 'The Window', an insert used in many church magazines.

It was during his time at the Priory and Parish Church that major problems were found with the fabric of the building. This resulted in having to remove the only remaining section of the 15th century timber in the roof of the building in 1962, because of wet-rot. The area was over St. Thomas' Chapel. New steel beams were put in and encased in oak boarding, so that they looked no different than before.

St. Peter's

St. Peter's became a Roman Catholic Cathedral in 1925, on the creation of the new Diocese of Lancaster in the Arch-Diocese of Liverpool.

One of the best-known buildings in the city, it was built in 1859 to the designs of local architect E. G. Paley, its graceful Gothic spire towering over the surrounding area.

With great ceremonial, and with a temporary throne in the chancel, the Right Rev. Thomas Wulstan Pearson was consecrated as Bishop in February 1925.

Thomas Pearson

Pearson was quite a character. In 1955, he bought a Lakeland mountainside, and with it a 1,250 ft. crag, farm buildings, 20 acres of farm land and scores of acres of fell in Great Langdale.

It was to become the permanent home of the Achille Ratti Climbing Club, which he had founded in 1942. His love of mountaineering went back to his days as a student in Rome when he climbed in the Alps and Appenines.

He took Mass on peaks in the Lake District and led a climb when Cardinal Griffin visited the Achille Ratti club hut in 1946. The club, first known as the Catholic Mountaineering Club, was later renamed Achille Ratti after Pope Pious XI, who as a young priest, was an expert Alpine climber.

The Presbytery pedestal

A curiously shaped stone pedestal at the entrance to St. Peter's has often aroused curiosity.

The stones were originally the topmost stones of the original cross of the Cathedral spire. The spire was the last part of the building to be completed, and the cross was fixed in position on September 14, 1859 – the Feast of the Holy Cross – three weeks before the consecration of the church. For 41 years, they surmounted the spire, standing four-square to the elements, at a height of 240 feet above sea level.

In 1900, the spire was repointed and the cross regilded, it then being discovered that the three top stones were split and decayed. They had to be removed and were replaced by others, forming the base of the cross of copper 8 ft 10 in high and 4 ft across. The old stones were built up in their original form and placed in the Presbytery garden.

Edmund Sharpe

Another leading church architect from Lancaster was Edmund Sharpe, who not only built many churches but did much to modernise the city.

Born in 1809 and educated at Cambridge, he took up architecture and travelled much in France and Germany. He came back to England in 1836, and practised as an architect for 15 years. 35 churches were designed by him, as well as several stately homes, his designs helping to revive the Gothic style in church architecture.

A Gold Medallist and Fellow of the Royal Institute of British Architects, he wrote several important books.

Sharpe was an extraordinarily energetic figure. He served on Lancaster Council from 1841 to 1853, becoming Mayor, and did much for the improvement of the sanitary condition of the town and the procurement of clean water.

Additionally, he promoted railways (including that to Morecambe), encouraged literary and scientific study, and was a keen musician and sportsman. He died in Milan in 1877.

Thomas Flynn

An outstanding Roman Catholic Churchman was the Right Rev. Thomas Edward Flynn, the city's second R. C. Bishop. He was elected to follow Pearson in 1939, when the diocese was only 19 years old.

Unfortunately for Flynn, less than two months after his consecration came the start of the Second World War, but after 1945, the diocese developed greatly under his leadership.

Parishes increased from 75 to nearly 100, including St. Bernadette's (see below). The Roman Catholic population rose from 97,000 to about 120,000, and the number of priests from 190 to nearly 260. There were nearly 50 Mass centres and no place of 1,000 inhabitants was without a weekly Mass. More convents were established, and a dozen new religious congregations joined the diocese.

Flynn was an interesting man. The eldest son of a family of five boys and a girl, his father, an orphaned Liverpudlian, was a Regular soldier, and his mother a convert to the Roman Catholic faith.

He was born at Portsmouth but only three weeks later the family moved to Warrington. Flynn's serious education began at St. Francis Xavier's School, Liverpool.

The story is told that when one of the Fathers asked him if he wanted to be a priest, he replied, *'No, Father, I want to be a Bishop'*.

He moved on to St. Edward's, Liverpool, as an ecclesiastical student and later won a scholarship to Cambridge, where he took the Natural Science Tripos. He then completed his formal education at Fribourg, with philosophy.

After parish work at various locations and teaching at St. Edward's College, Ware, and Upholland, where he became Headmaster and Professor of Philosophy, he was recalled to parish work in 1932, when he became parish priest of St. Mary's, Chorley.

After a preaching tour of America, he became a canon and Dean of Chorley and in 1939 was elected Bishop of Lancaster. Flynn died in 1961.

St. John's Chapel

One of the best known, but unfortunately little-used churches which provides a prominent feature on Lancaster's skyline is St. John's, on North Road, built in 1754.

The church started life as a chapel-of-ease to the Priory and Parish Church and originally was called Green Ayre Chapel. All fees were reserved for the Vicar of St. Mary's, to whom marriages, christenings and burials at the new chapel had to be reported.

For the building of the chapel, £820 was left by Dr. William Stratford; Francis Reynolds and Edward Marton, MPs for the Borough, gave £205, and other *'pious and well-disposed persons'* gave £300.

Three years after its building, the chapel was enlarged.

From the start there was a close association between Lancaster Corporation and St. John's. In May 1749, the Corporation agreed to allot land for the chapel and to give £100, later increased to £200. It was resolved that the Mayor and Bailiffs should join in soliciting subscriptions from private people, and the Corporation built the church's two galleries.

Modern Buildings

It is not only the great church buildings of Lancaster that are impressive. Some of the newer ones are too, though not necessarily for architectural reasons.

St. Bernadette's

Go to Bowerham and you will find St. Bernadette's, opened in 1958. It is a striking enough building, which, until recently, had an 80 ft tall, slender tower, but the really inspiring story of this church is the faith shown by its congregation.

Work started on this modern-style building in September 1956. The foundation stone was laid and blessed by the Roman Catholic Bishop of Lancaster, the Right Rev. T. E. Flynn, in February 1957. The opening of the church in May 1958 marked the culmination of determined work by the congregation in getting the church they needed to replace a former converted barn.

St. Bernadette's came into being in 1948 as a chapel-of-ease to the Cathedral, St. Peter's. However, in September 1953, it was created a separate entity, with Father C. Aspinall as priest. What was needed was a church to cope with a rapidly increasing congregation, and they toiled in all manner of ways to raise money for the new church.

Efforts included the collection of scrap metal, waste paper and firewood as the congregation met the challenge. They even established a salvage department in 1956, one of the members of the congregation taking out a licence as a metal broker. A lesson in practical, no-nonsense Faith.

Church to Theatre – St. Anne's

One of the most interesting churches in Lancaster is today not a church at all, for the former St. Anne's Church, in Moor Lane, is now the Duke's Theatre. At one time, it was one of the most popular churches in Lancaster, but times change, populations and social values shift, and by the late 1950s St. Anne's closed, and the parish became a united benefice with St. John's.

The redevelopment schemes of the 1950s were what really led to the demise of St.

Reflections on Lancaster

The Duke's Playhouse – imaginative use of the old St. Anne's Church

Anne's as a church. A huge amount of demolition took place in the area, much of the new building taking years to materialise, and the area went into decline. With the joining of St. Anne's and St. John's, the new parish had a population of about 7,300. The boundaries included Penny Street, Dalton Square, Edward Street, Ridge and Newton Estates, the Bulk area, Parliament Street and Cable Street.

However, when St. Anne's closed its doors late in 1958, although it caused a great deal of sadness to some parishioners, it was not unexpected.

The suggestion that St. Anne's should be closed and the parish added to St. John's had been made as long ago as 1918. In 1923, a public inquiry was held into the proposed union of the benefices and a report made to the Bishop of Manchester. The report recommended the unification, with St. John's as the parish church, and the demolition of St. Anne's. The site and materials were to be sold, and the proceeds to be used for the building of a new church on the outskirts of the town. There was great opposition and the scheme petered out.

Again, in 1928, the Ecclesiastical Commissioners recommended the union of St. Anne's and St. John's. However, there was strong opposition from St. Anne's, who eventually took the case to the Privy Council and the objection was upheld.

The closure in 1958 brought to an end a distinguished history dating back to 1796. In the Baptismal Register is an entry of January 26, 1843 – the date of Lord Ashton's baptism.

Robert Housman

The founder of the church had been a native of Lancaster, the Rev. Robert Housman, who until 1786, had conducted services at St. John's – (perhaps St. John's had always had its eyes on St. Anne's!). He then took over a new post in Leicester, but visiting Lancaster eight years later with his second wife, Jane, (he was formerly married to Agnes Gunson, of Millom), he decided to leave the Midlands and build a church of his own in Lancaster.

Printed circulars were issued concerning the project and generous assistance was given by a hard-working group of townsfolk. The scheme blossomed in August 1796, when the Bishop of Chester consecrated the church. Housman was the first Vicar and served with distinction for more than 40 years.

At the time of the unification of St. Anne's and St. John's, there were suggestions that St. John's Church should be rebuilt on what was then the new Ridge estate.

5

Horses, The Sands and World War II

Horses and Traffic

Some of the great changes in life slide by almost unnoticed at the time. For instance, the last horse in the Highways Department of the City Council – where once there had been scores – was sold in September 1949, making the Department completely mechanised.

An earnest Councillor assured a meeting of the Council that the horse had been sold to a good home and would not go for horsemeat. The loss of horses from the streets and agriculture often brings expressions of regret. But do those who regret the change remember things the way they were really?

The streets of Lancaster were often congested with horse-carriages and other horse-drawn vehicles as much as they are today with motor traffic, and on a hot summer's day it became all too apparent that horses produce large and pungent amounts of environmentally-friendly material.

Many were the family who sent 'our kid' out after horses had gone by to collect the free donations of manure that littered the roads. Very useful for the garden and allotment.

Traffic of one kind or another has always been a problem in Lancaster. It took many years of campaigning before a bridge (Greyhound Bridge) was used to relieve the endless flow of vehicles over Skerton Bridge. The vast expansion of car ownership since the 1950s means that today two questions occupy the mind. What is the meaning of Life? Where am I going to park?

It is nothing new, of course. Only a year after the end of the Second World War, Lancaster traders complained in the Lancaster Guardian that motorists were blocking the narrow streets with inconsiderate and careless parking, cluttering up the shop fronts, even when not making purchases, and members of the public complained that Market Street, New Street and Church Street in particular were becoming 'death traps'.

The Boundary Riding

Every seven years, Lancaster formerly held its Boundary Riding, a colourful event that unfortunately has disappeared from the civic calendar, as the grey blanket of 1974 local government reorganisation covered the area.

But much of the colour from this occasion started to disappear even before the Second World War. In 1935, the Council decided that motor cars would be used instead of horses and carriages. Although some horses were still being used in the 1950s, the occasion was not the spectacle that it had been formerly.

The really early boundary ridings must have been quite something. In 1809, it was reported that,

'The Mayor and Bailiffs of this Borough, accompanied by a great number of gentlemen, on horseback, made their septennial perambulation of the boundaries. About noon they partook of a cold collation on the Moor, at a place called the Red Moss Well, near to Claugha (sic) Pike – "God Save the King" was sung in great stile with three times three several other loyal and constitutional songs were also given. On their return in the evening, they were met on the Caton road by the officers belonging to the Friendly Societies, with their flags, who preceded them into the town, and on their arrival in the Market Place, "God Save the King" was again sung with three times three, and the company separated, much pleased with the attention which had been paid to them during the whole of the day by the Mayor and Bailiffs.'

The Friendly Societies

At this time there were 13 male Friendly Societies in the town, involving over 2,000 members, and three female societies, involving just over 200 members. The names of the societies were redolent of the times.

A colourful ceremony from the past – the Boundary Riding

The male societies were: Friendship and Unity, Unity, Unanimous, Loyal Union, Provident, Benevolent, Friendly, Union, Humane, Amicable, Brotherly, Samaritan and Good Intent. The female societies were Amicable, Benevolent and Friendly.

The Sands

It's very easy to get the charms of the past out of perspective. Modes of transport are a good case in point. One can just picture in the mind's eye the days of our forefathers journeying by stage coach – the ladies dressed in the fashion of the times, looking, we are led to believe, very demure, and the gentlemen very courteous – so say the historians who adhere to the Christmas card image of times past.

In fact, those old stage coaches were far from comfortable. Lack of heating meant many layers of clothing were required by the traveller. All of the coaches were of ponderous strength, some resting bodily on the axle. Early forms of suspension being primitive, the passengers were jolted and jerked the entire journey.

One historian has it that the first stage coach to be seen in this district, about 1763, was drawn by six horses, and went by the name of 'The Flying Machine'. Before the building of Skerton Bridge in the late 1700s, the stage coaches came rumbling over the pot-holed, rutted, muddy roads of old China Street, down Bridge Lane and across an old and decrepit bridge. Then, on towards the foot of Bridge Lane and St. George's Quay, into Lune Street, Skerton, up Main Street and on to Halton Road to the North, via Slyne.

Here came the left turning to Hest Bank,

Reflections on Lancaster

where the short but treacherous journey across the Sands started. This was the Oversands route to Grange and Cartmel, instead of the long way round Carnforth and Milnthorpe.

Tragedy was a frequent event on this route across the Sands. Many churchyards in the neighbourhood bear witness to the fact, as coaches tried to beat fast, incoming tides and shifting, water-logged sands. In 1857, for instance, seven farm workers were drowned, but this was the year that the Furness Railway was opened and the Oversands route was discontinued on any regular basis.

There is now an official Guide to this treacherous route, which is still walked. One story is told of an ancient mariner who, when asked if Guides were ever lost on the sands, replied:

'I never knew any lost. There's one or two drowned now and again, but they are generally found when the tide goes out.'

Hooligans and Vandals

As a reminder that hooligans and vandals have always been with us, it is recorded that on the night of April 30, 1812, some evil-disposed persons placed nearly a dozen obstructions across the road between Lancaster and Burton-in-Kendal, with the apparent intention of upsetting the stage coach. Some things never change.

The reasons for this kind of behaviour remain a mystery to this day, of course. Television programmes are blamed. The cinema is blamed. Couldn't-care-less parents are blamed. The education system is blamed. Everything and everyone is blamed, except the offenders. In the early years of the present century, *'pernicious literature'* was blamed. The newspaper The Visitor, at Morecambe, thundered on about a case at Lancaster Quarter Sessions.

'These filthy books give the young mind the most extraordinary ideas, and they get so infatuated that they endeavour to imitate the tricks of mystic characters.'

The purple prose continued:

'It is all right to be imaginative, but not as the result of the influence of these Deadwood Dicks. Parents should keep an eye on what their young hopefuls are reading. They haven't as much regard for the Sabbath as boys in the worst of Slumdon. Alas, the majority of the parents do not care two straws what they do, how they behave, or how they annoy others ... Instead of receiving a good horsewhipping ... as was administered in

the days of old, they are merely laughed at and considered roguish.'

Somehow there seems to be a topical flavour to all this, despite the passage of nearly 80 years.

Folklore

It is the stated intention of this book not to delve too far back into the city's past, but to concentrate on more recent times. However, some stories of the old city are irresistible, and have entered the local folklore.

John Charnley

One case is that of the Charnley family, and in particular that of John Charnley, in command of the *'Thetis'*. The officer fell in with the French privateer 'Buonaparte' about November 8, 1804. The French vessel held 16 or 18 guns and was manned by 215 men. Four times did the gallant Captain Charnley repulse the French. Two of his men were killed and five wounded.

The inhabitants of St. Dominica presented him with a piece of plate and £240 to be divided among his crew for bravely beating off the French with only 45 men against 215. For many years afterwards, pupils at Lancaster Royal Grammar School sang a ditty in praise of Captain Charnley, who died in November 1834, aged 64.

These were the days when Lancaster was a seafaring town full of old seasalts who would spin many wonderful yarns (some true!) about their adventures. They were colourful characters who could have stepped out of the pages of 'Treasure Island'.

Slave trade

In the 18th century, a chief trading route for the sea dogs was to the West Indies and Africa – meaning that a considerable part of Lancaster's wealth emanated from the slave trade.

At one period, there were 14 vessels sailing from Lancaster engaged in this trade, euphemistically referred to as the 'Black Ivory' trade. Romance and legend have woven round this cruel period in history. It is difficult – sometimes impossible – to separate fact from fiction.

One story is that a Captain Marshall stole a Guinea King's daughter, and that this finished any further dealings with the Lancaster traders. A likely story! More probable that it was the campaigning of Wilberforce and his anti-slavery society . . . but one never knows.

In the slave trade, the voyage was

'three-cornered'. The ships sailed to the west coast of Africa where they shipped the slaves from depots where their living freight had been forcibly rounded up. Then it was on to the West Indies, where the slaves were sold.

The proceeds were brought home as cargoes of such things as sugar, rum and mahogany. So plentiful was this expensive wood in Lancaster, that examples of its use could be found in the houses of the humble as well as the grand.

The Second World War

Lancaster in the Second World War escaped lightly, very few bombs falling on the city, and consequently little damage. The nearness of the military target of Barrow-in-Furness was one of the reasons for Lancaster's good fortune.

For a whole year Lancaster escaped any damage at all. It was not until the night of August 31, 1940, that the first 'visitation' by enemy bombers produced 'results'. At 11.20 pm, incendiary bombs fell in the Bowerham district. About the same time, it was reported that two flares had been dropped, and aircraft were heard circling overhead.

Altogether, 50 bombs were accounted for. Of these, 12 fell on houses, 17 in gardens and nine in roadways. Miraculously, there was only one casualty, a 17-year-old youth with a lack of Air Raid Precautions knowledge who attempted to deal with a bomb by throwing water on it. He was overcome by the fumes which resulted and collapsed.

Interestingly, the museum in the Old Town Hall, (which had been closed on September 2, 1939, and did not re-open until 1947), was for part of the Second World War offices of the Canadian Treasury. Who knows what sensitive secrets were stored in the cellars?

Post-War Times

Mention is made in Chapter Seven of the great part women have played in the history of Lancaster. But it was as late as 1945 before women police were seen for the first time on the streets of the city. The then Chief Constable, William Thompson, went to great lengths to tell a committee:

'The three members of the Women's Auxiliary Police Corps have undergone a course of basic training, lasting six weeks, at the Lancashire County Police Women's Training School at Salesbury, and the knowledge gained will no doubt be extremely useful to them in the efficient discharge of their duties and will

have given them an insight into the nature of the tasks which they may be called upon to perform.'

Housing

After the end of the Second World War, and through the Fifties, Sixties and Seventies, the face of Lancaster changed greatly. Great swathes of the town were redeveloped. Many rows of terraced houses were torn down, on a few occasions to be replaced by non-descript blocks of flats and large council housing estates.

It is easy now, with the benefit of hindsight, to blame the city fathers for some of the less than satisfactory building that went on, but public authorities were under pressure.

In the Fifties it was the Age of Austerity. One could scarcely put one brick on top of another without having to have a licence.

Furthermore, adequate supplies of building materials were as rare as a Seventh Day Adventist working among journalists.

An army of bureaucrats wound so much red tape around every transaction that it is surprising that many of the buildings even rose from their foundations.

There were huge social problems, not the least of which was housing, so the civic fathers had to build. They had to build with what they could get hold of and in the most economic way possible to make housing accessible to all. We should not blame them too much for some of their mistakes. Some of the problems were insoluble.

13 Children!

Many families tended to be larger than nowadays, though few were as large as one Skerton family. When they put in their claim for the newly-established Family Allowance, they created what may well remain a record.

The parents had 13 children. Their eldest son was serving in India with the RAF and their eldest daughter was employed in Lancaster, so the claim was in respect of the remaining eleven. Included in the eleven were four sets of twins.

'Answers' to the problems

The housing estates and blocks of flats were sorely needed, the Council did the best they could at the time, and indeed there was considerable pride when some of the developments came into being.

The 11-storey blocks of flats at Mainway, Skerton, opened in 1960. They replaced former run-down terraced housing and were opened by Dame Evelyn Sharp,

Permanent Secretary to the Ministry of Housing and Local Government. She described the scheme as a magnificent housing development. Not only did she commend the building of blocks of flats as high as eleven storeys, she urged the Corporation in future to consider building higher, to 20 or even 30 storeys. It was, she said, a new departure for one of the oldest and most famous cities in the country. Incoming tenants might feel a little strange after living in normal-type houses, but they would soon become intensely proud of their new homes.

Queueing for Everything

Of the immediate post-Second World War years, life for many was a little grey because of rationing. It seemed to go on for ever and interfere with almost every part of life. Unless one was fortunate enough to be able to acquire goods 'under the counter', from a variety of 'spivs' or other 'just this side of the law' dubious characters, these were straitened times.

A rumour of goods available could start a rush. Knowledge that goods were available could almost automatically start a queue. You queued for everything.

So great were the queues at Lancaster bus station on the day a multiple store opened in Morecambe, that extra buses had to be put on and a five minute service was operated between 11 am and 3 pm. What were the articles of attraction? Nylon stockings, rubber hot-water bottles and alarm clocks.

Entertainment

At least in those days there was a lively entertainment scene. The cinema was a way of life and just about everyone went to a weekly dance, with 'live' music. There were dozens of local groups of musicians.

The 'Harmony Hawaiians'

Who now remembers Tony Troughton and His Harmony Hawaiians, who hit the local scene in 1937, and claimed to be the first combination to feature electric guitars in the North! The group, which became very well known and made at least one broadcast, was formed by Tony Troughton, who lived in Ashton Drive. Unfortunately, the War interfered with their progress. In September 1939, the band had fixed up a series of variety bookings, and were due to open in Southport on September 4 – but a certain event occurred the previous day to put a stop to this.

Instrumentalists and vocalists – notably

two brothers Williams serving in the Territorials were immediately mobilised to fulfil engagements in war theatres all over the world.

Tony formed another outfit which succeeded in getting a broadcast in September 1941, which yielded another crop of engagements, but again, the war intervened and personnel were called up.

Until the end of hostilities, Tony carried on alone, developing an individual act, the highlight of which was an interpretation of a bombing raid at sea, done with the aid of an electric guitar.

He played to war workers and wounded all over the country and became associated in the process with leading variety stars including Max Miller, Issy Bonn and Caroll Lewis.

The line-up of the band in 1947 was: Tony Troughton, Ted Sears, Gordon Wilton (guitars), Lauri Horrobin (bass), Jeff Smith (solo plectrum guitar), Ronnie Williams (vocalist and hula drums), Jack Renhall (uke), and Edith Bradley (vocalist), the last three named, being known as the Harmony Trio. Happy Days!

Demise of the County Club

The decades after the war saw many old institutions swept away as society changed. Few could illustrate the change more graphically than the demise in 1958 of the old Lancaster County Club, which had existed since 1873.

The city's most exclusive club, it had included in its membership those male members of county families who lived in the district, the holders of high office in State and County, and prominent professional men. Its guests over the years included distinguished Judges, politicians, Church dignitaries and foreign diplomats. But times change, the old order was being swept away, and by the 1950s the lofty and impressive dining room, the bedrooms and the games rooms were being but little used.

The Club had started its life at Great John Street, but after a decade moved to Church Street. There were some great characters associated with it. William Rose, who when the Club closed was 79, had been steward for 36 years, following his father, who had held the position for 46 years. Rose was a survivor of the sinking of the Lusitania. Another character was D. P. Sturton, a Lancaster solicitor aged over 80 at the time of the closure, who was secretary for over 50 years until he retired in 1957.

'Greener' Lancaster

Because of its former great industries, Lancaster of the past had a skyline of tall, smoke-belching chimneys. Virtually all of them have gone, and the city is a cleaner, or to use the modern jargon, 'more environmentally-friendly', place.

But another great change had an equal impact in achieving this new cleanliness. Until the 1960s, coal was the fuel of Everyman. Thousands of domestic chimneys dumped their smoke into the air. That started coming to an end in the early Sixties, when the first Smoke Control Orders were approved. The first area involved was small, but important. It was roughly bounded by George Street and Spring Garden Street on the South side, Dalton Square, Rosemary Lane and Chapel Street to the East, Cable Street on the North side and Bridge Lane, China Street and King Street in the West.

Miss World

Indeed, life probably changed more in the 1960s for the general people of Lancaster than it had at any time before. Even a girl from a relatively humble background in Lancaster could rise to become 'Miss World'. That is what 18-year-old Rosemarie Frankland, of Granville Road, did in the Autumn of 1961.

Rosemarie launched into a glittering world and marriage (though later divorce) to the night picture editor of the old Daily Sketch. In those pre-Women's Lib days all newspaper reporters were expected to know the 'vital statistics' of beauty queens, and it was with some relish that local and national papers reported that 36-22-36 Rosemarie, former store assistant in Lancaster, had won the title.

Before 1961 was out, she flew to Hollywood and toured with Bob Hope, entertaining American troops. The Cinderella story of a girl who only a year before had been selling socks in a Lancaster store. It wouldn't have happened in grandmother's day!

6

The White Lund Explosion

Between Lancaster and Morecambe lies the White Lund Industrial Estate, an enterprise started jointly by the two local authorities many years ago. Few who visit the area today realise that it was once the scene of almost indescribable horror during a night in which many died and scores of others were injured in the most appalling circumstances. There had been a huge munitions factory here, which literally blew up one night.

The fateful night was October 1, 1917. The vast shellfilling factory, constructed under Lloyd George's regime at the Ministry of Munitions, employed thousands filling shells made at the Lancaster National Projectile Factory.

Suddenly, without warning, there was a series of explosions sending shells screaming through the air, casting a lurid glow in the night sky and filling the streets of Morecambe with panic-stricken men, women and children who thought the area was under attack.

Many of the factory's workers were killed and injured, and the factory virtually wiped off the map. The glare from the fires could be seen from as far away as Barrow-in-Furness, on the other side of Morecambe Bay. Explosions were heard at Burnley, over 40 miles away in East Lancashire, and throughout the Lancaster and Morecambe district, hundreds of windows shattered in the force of the blasts.

The cause was never fully established. Some said it was the work of German spies (the country was going through spy hysteria), others that it was sheer accident. However, because of wartime censorship of the Press, few people outside the immediate area got to know of the full horror of that tragic night, for all that appeared in newspapers even two days later was, *'Explosion at North of England Munition Works. Factory gutted. No deaths as yet reported'*.

The disaster could well have had something to do with the fact that the White Lund factory was built at almost incredible speed. Within only three months, the former farm land became covered in buildings, and the filling of the first shell was said to have been carried out only 14 weeks after the decision to build had

Reflections on Lancaster

Workers at Lancaster's First World War National Projectile Factory

50

Reflections on Lancaster

been made.

Prior to the explosion there was a reminder of the land's former agricultural use. One of the treasures of the mostly women employees, was an apple tree, the only one remaining out of former large orchards. The tree stood between two of the high-explosive sheds and its fruit was jealously guarded. Around the factory, in their spare time, the women cultivated allotments, providing most of the vegetables for the canteen.

Perhaps it had been tempting fate that the White Lund Munitions Factory was designated 'Number 13'.

When White Lund blew up, the scene was terrifying. Men, women and children, some not waiting to throw a coat over their scanty night attire, fled from their homes. In Morecambe, some made for the beach, others for the villages of Bolton-le-Sands, Hest Bank and Slyne – anywhere to get out of reach of the shells hurtling through the air. Some took to boats to take them out into Morecambe Bay, but even there they were not safe, for shells fell miles out at sea.

The rescue parties had a dreadful task in locating and identifying the dead and injured. To make matters worse, the local hospital was hopelessly inadequate. Mattresses were laid on floors for the injured. Explosions took place even as the rescuers combed through the wreckage. One man commented,

'Suddenly there was a flare which lit up the heavens for miles around, followed by a terrific, deafening explosion. I was lifted clean off my feet and carried through the air, how far I cannot tell, but when I recovered I found myself in a ditch of water, my clothes torn to rags and covered with mud. I was wet to the skin and my lips and nose were bleeding.' Another said, *'Women were moaning for their husbands and relatives ... Terror-stricken children were crying.'*

Confusion

The first explosions started at about 9.45 pm on the bright, moonlit night. Fire Brigades from throughout the North West were called but with tons of explosives at the seats of the fires, the situation was virtually helpless.

Even to this day there is some confusion about the number of deaths on that terrible night. Wartime censorship played down all information. Some give the death toll as eleven, others as high as 16, but both figures would be miraculously low. Confusion would also arise between how many actually died on the spot, and how many died later of injuries.

The disaster was followed by an inquest on the victims, and it speaks volumes for the safety measures of those days, that the recommendations made, seem blindingly obvious nowadays:

> *'That if the factory is rebuilt, radiating exits should be provided; that all gates should be made to open both ways without obstruction; that arrangements be made for efficient cut-offs in the run-ways; that all buildings be supplied with sprinklers, and that they be automatic; and that as little wood or other inflammable material as possible be used for constructional purposes.'*

Disaster strikes again

The factory reopened after the First World War but even then, claimed more lives. The workers were no longer filling shells but defusing and emptying them. On January 14, 1920, an explosion took place and nine men lost their lives. One of them, Wilfred Walker, of Heysham, had escaped the 1917 disaster.

Today, all vestiges of these horrific scenes have been swept away. Occasionally, rusting shells and pieces of ironwork surface during excavations for building, but now, White Lund is a growing industrial estate. At its maximum output, the number of employees at the White Lund Munitions Works totalled 4,500. The wages paid to them reached the then astronomical amount of over £8,000 a week.

National Projectile Factory

The other great munitions works in the area, was the National Projectile Factory, on Caton Road. Much of the old industrial building along Caton Road dates from the Wagon Works. This made trams and railway rolling stock, and in the First World War, was taken over to house German prisoners-of-war, many of whom were employed in making the new road, Kingsway, which led to the National Projectile Factory.

George V and Queen Mary visited the Lancaster factory, which employed between 7,000 and 9,000, on May 16, 1917, the same day that they visited the ill-fated White Lund factory.

At the height of its production, the National Projectile Factory employed over 4,000 women, who must have found earning high wages an exhilarating experience. No doubt, it was also a salutary lesson in female liberation for the men working alongside them. But the end of the First World War saw the

The old Power Station in Caton Road

Reflections on Lancaster

end of the necessity for the factory.

> 'The services of many thousands of employees, whose combined efforts with up-to-date machinery have resulted in such a wonderful output of shells during the past three years, were dispensed with at the Christmas holidays',

reported the newspaper 'The Visitor' in January 1919. A few employees were kept on, closure coming finally in mid-1921.

Change to Power

The area became the site of a Power Station, more correctly a generating station, demolished only a few years ago after it ceased generating in 1977. Its 250 ft high chimney was a landmark for miles. The Power Station played a crucial role during the Second World War when, amidst considerable secrecy, £1,000,000 was spent on its extension and two 20,000 kilowatt sets installed. The installation of the first of these was started in 1940, and the second was a war emergency extension to meet increased industrial demands, and to provide against other plants in the North West being bombed. A third set was visualised but proved unnecessary.

The Caton Road Power Station achieved almost legendary efficiency, even though it operated with wartime shortages. The

Reflections on Lancaster

boilers were designed to burn fair-quality Lancashire and Yorkshire slacks, and although two particular coals were specified, because of the war the station had to use 70 different kinds of fuel. The 250 ft high chimney was impressive, with an 11 ft 6 in internal diameter at the top, and the boiler house roof was 82 ft above ground level.

For many years, the station supplied both Lancaster and Morecambe areas and the surrounding villages. It was formally opened in 1924 and took over from Lancaster's first power station, which had been built in Marton Road, in 1893. 'The Visitor' newspaper commented, on the opening of the Caton Road works, that they were

> *'the outcome of a broad-minded and visionary policy of the Lancaster Corporation to provide a station which will adequately meet the needs of the two boroughs of Morecambe and Lancaster, and the Urban District of Heysham, and also to supply the whole district within 20 miles of Lancaster as and when such a service is required.'*

The station cost about £70,000 to build and equip.

7

'Lancaster Worthies'

How does one choose fairly who to mention out of the thousands of people associated with Lancaster who have 'made their mark' on even the recent history of the city? The answer is that with only limited space available, it is not possible. Therefore, the selection must be something of a lottery, the full story of latter-day 'Lancaster Worthies' being saved for a future occasion.

Medical Men

Many medical men have come from the Lancaster area, and many others have 'adopted' the city, Lancaster having several major hospitals being not the least of the reasons for this.

Sir Herbert Barker

One colourful character identified with Lancaster was Sir Herbert Barker, who ended his days here after an unfortunate accident when he stumbled and fell getting out of a car, fracturing his thigh. Sir Herbert Barker became one of the most famous manipulative surgeons of his day.

He died in 1950, at the age of 81, the accident happening while he was holidaying at the home of his sister at Burton, Westmorland. By this time he had become a well-known figure throughout Lancashire.

He was born at Southport, the son of Thomas Wildman Barker, lawyer and coroner for South West Lancashire, and although trained for the legal profession, went against family expectations and showed marked ability for manipulative surgery.

He had a distinguished career, receiving his knighthood in 1922, giving a demonstration of his methods to the British Orthopaedic Association at St. Thomas' Hospital, in 1936, and making a series of films in 1939 for perpetuation of his technique. Many artists and literary men were among his friends and a portrait of him was painted by Augustus John.

Lady Jane Ethel Barker, his widow, died in 1959 while living in Kent. She was renowned for her beauty, charm and kindness and was ever at her husband's side at his clinic in Park Lane, London, and on his numerous visits to New York and other American and Continental cities.

Origins of the Plastic Eye

Lancaster lays claim to having been the home of the inventor of the plastic eye. William Barker (no relation of the above), inventor of the eye, lived at 12, Ashton Drive.

Educated at the local National School (the 'Nashy' as it was known throughout Lancaster), and Lancaster Royal Grammar School, Barker entered the then revolutionary world of plastics, when he was a dental mechanic in the city. He heard a lecture by a German doctor on plastics in dentistry and perfected the eye while working for a Kendal dentist in 1942. It then went on to be developed throughout the world.

It was perhaps ironic that it should have been a German who inspired him to this work. In 1945, he was placed in charge of the Ministry of Pensions Plastic Eye Unit at Norcross, Blackpool, where he was responsible for the supply of plastic eyes to war pensioners. Later, with the National Health Service, the work was extended to civilians and plastic eye centres opening throughout the country.

The Cassidy's

One of the great 'medical names' of Lancaster is Cassidy, for both father and son received much public recognition. In 1949, when the King was ill, among those attending was Sir Maurice Alan Cassidy. His father, Dr. David Mackay Cassidy, had for many years been Medical Superintendent at the County Mental Hospital, later named the Lancaster Moor Hospital. Educated at Lancaster Royal Grammar School, Sir Maurice became Physician Extraordinary to George V in 1932, and in 1937, Physician to the King.

His rise to fame was rapid. After leaving the Royal Grammar School he went to Clare College, Cambridge, and then to St. Thomas' Hospital. In the King's 1934 New Year Honours, he received the distinction of Knight Commander of the Royal Victorian Order, for conspicuous service to medical science. Sir Maurice died in 1949, only a month or so after treating the King. A short time before his death he received the G.C.V.O. at the hands of the King at his home – a rare extra honour falling to him by the King calling upon him.

Sir Montagu John Eddy

A 20th century railway pioneer was also associated with Lancaster. Sir Montagu John Eddy started his distinguished railway career in the city, where he was Assistant Superintendent. He married

Dorothy Hilda Hall, daughter of Dr. William Hall, of Lancaster, and went to Buenos Aires, where he eventually became chairman of the Great Southern Railway Company, until it was taken over by the Argentinian Government.

Eddy returned to Britain and, although a director of other Argentine railways, during the Second World War became Deputy Chairman of the Prisoners-of-War Department of the British Red Cross Society.

Lawyers

Sir Lancelot Sanderson

Among many lawyers associated with Lancaster was Sir Lancelot Sanderson, P.C., K.C., who became Chief Justice of Bengal. He was a popular figure in the North West until his death in 1944. Born in Lancaster in 1863, he came of a Westmorland family who had lived for many generations near Great Strickland.

Sanderson started life with the proverbial Silver Spoon, having a banking and legal background from the start. His father John was general manager of the old Lancaster Banking Company, and his elder brother was J. Tunstall Sanderson, Clerk to the South Lonsdale and Garstang, and Morecambe and Heysham Magistrates.

Educated at Elstree and Harrow, he was an outstanding student at Cambridge and entered the Inner Temple on choosing the Bar as his profession.

He rapidly made a name for himself on the Northern Circuit at Lancaster Assizes and Quarter Sessions especially.

Becoming a King's Counsel in 1903, nine years later he was elected a Bencher of the Inner Temple. In 1915, he was appointed Chief Justice of Calcutta, a month after the appointment receiving his knighthood.

He became Chief Justice of Bengal and a Vice-Chancellor of Calcutta University, but then his wife became fatally ill and he resigned his Bengal appointment in 1926, his wife dying only a few hours after he arrived home.

Later that year, he was appointed a member of the Privy Council and the Lord Chancellor placed him on the Judicial Committee.

A 'local boy made good' story indeed, but Sanderson also had a considerable political career, representing North Westmorland as Conservative MP in the Commons, from 1910 to 1915.

Other aspects of this man include his appointment as chairman of the Lancaster Quarter Sessions in 1927, (later becoming chairman of the Westmorland Quarter Sessions as well), and appointment as a Commissioner of Assize in 1931. He was also closely involved in sport at national and local level – at one time, vice-chairman of the M.C.C.

Sir John Edward Singleton

Another leading lawyer was Sir John Edward Singleton, Kt., who became a Judge of the King's Bench Division in 1934, and in 1948, was appointed a Lord Justice of Appeal.

Born at Churchtown, near Garstang, Sir John received his early education at Lancaster Royal Grammar School (the Singleton House at the school being named after him), before going on to Pembroke College, Cambridge.

He was called to the Bar of the Inner Temple in 1906, became a King's Counsel in 1922, and was Conservative MP for Lancaster 1922-23. In 1929, he was elected a Bencher of the Inner Temple.

During the First World War, Sanderson served in France and Belgium in the H.F.A, and was mentioned in despatches.

From 1928 to 1934, he was Recorder of Preston, and during the same period, up to 1933, was Judge of Appeal, Isle of Man.

In 1936, he was Judge at Manchester Assizes at the trial of the Parsee-Indian Lancaster, Dr Buck Ruxton, sentencing him to death for the murder of his wife Isobel and maid, Mary Rogerson.

Chocolate connection

A little-known commercial link in Lancaster is that with the Cadbury chocolate company. John Cadbury, founder of Cadbury Bros., of Bourneville, had many associations with Lancaster through his second marriage in 1832 to Candia

Barrow, daughter of George Barrow, of Lancaster, a wealthy shipowner and foreign merchant.

This marriage led to his close association and friendship with Richard Cadbury Barrow, who served as Mayor of Birmingham; John Cadbury, who died in 1889, at the age of 88, and began his career as a tea and coffee merchant in 1824, later establishing a cocoa and chocolate factory in Birmingham with his brother. He lived to see the Cadbury works employing over 1,200.

Margaret Bond

Women have played an influential part in the city's history. Typical was Margaret Bond, who lived at Bridge House and died, in her 88th year, in 1949.

The health of many of the city's youngsters owed a lot to her, for she promoted all forms of sport, being one of the foremost swimmers, skaters, golfers and tennis players in the district, and she encouraged the city's youngsters to take part.

She was a much-loved figure in Lancaster, and there are many who remember her elocution lessons, and when she entertained schoolchildren to cinema performances. These were always linked with an address, designed to impress upon her young guests the importance of religious and moral standards.

Motor Industry links

Sir Barton Townley

Giants of the North West motor industry are associated particularly with Lancaster. One such man was Sir Barton Townley, who lived at Bailrigg, now the University of Lancaster. He sold Bailrigg House and the surrounding farmland so that the campus could be built there in the early 1960s.

Townley's generosity seemed boundless. On several occasions, he financially helped the former Friends' School, he was a staunch Methodist, regularly attending Quernmore Methodist Church, and was a generous benefactor of many other causes. He died, aged 92, in 1981, his story being one of the business romances of Lancaster.

Barton Townley's father was a butcher in Lancaster and after Barton left school he started as a butcher's boy. But he was more interested in anything on wheels, although at that time, 1906, motoring and motorcycling were still in their infancy. Barton Townley was so 'motor mad' that some Lancaster people with cars used to drive to the butcher's shop for the youngster to put right problems with their vehicles.

The young Townley saved until he had enough to open a small cycle shop, with a few motorcycles in addition, in Penny Street. In 1911, he opened a garage further up the same street and then bought a prominent block of property at the apex of Penny Street and King Street. This set him up as a 'serious' motor car dealer, and he also bought or rented other premises in Lancaster and Morecambe.

Townley is credited with being the first motor dealer in the North West to start taking secondhand cars in exchange deals for new ones. Up to the early 1920s, motor car owners had the problem of selling their old car, when they wanted a new car. Barton Townley, with considerable foresight and business acumen, came to their rescue by giving allowances.

He built up an army of representatives who were sent all over Lancashire and Cumbria, depots opening at Preston, Blackpool, Blackburn, Barrow-in-Furness and Windermere.

The Second World War stifled the car trade, but the firm kept busy by maintaining agricultural and Forces machinery and vehicles. The post-War period saw a boom in motoring, once the petrol ration was taken off.

By the late 1940s, Barton Townley controlled eleven companies, trading under an 'umbrella' company, Northern Commercial Vehicles. Local readers will remember at least some of the names of those companies: Townley Motors Ltd., Blackburn; William Atkinson and Son, Lancaster; Standard and Triumph (Services) Ltd., Lancaster; Northern Vehicle Repairs, Lancaster; Croft and Ewans, Agricultural Engineers, Lancaster; Ford Depot, Lancaster; Austin Dealers, Lancaster; Barton Motors Ltd., Preston; Imperial Garages Ltd., Blackpool; Bowness Motors Ltd., Windermere; Barton Townley Ltd., Barrow-in-Furness. The yearly turnover of the companies ran into hundreds of thousands of pounds.

But Townley avoided having all his eggs in one basket. He was chairman of the Aldcliffe Hall Estate, Lancaster, owning several farms, land and property, and the Sylvan Estates, Lancaster, which had farms in, amongst other places, Grange-over-Sands, Carlisle and Garstang areas.

He also had many hundreds of thousands of pounds invested in South Africa, and was a frequent visitor to that troubled country. A larger-than-life character in the motor trade, he was modest about his many gifts to churches and schools, and he made nought of the fact that he anonymously helped many

Bailrigg, home of Barton Townley, motor magnate, who sold it to establish Lancaster University

lame dogs.

The timbered mansion of Bailrigg, two miles south of Lancaster, was his pride and joy. It was built in 1900 by Herbert Lushington Storey, and later acquired by Sir James Travis Clegg, chairman of Lancashire County Council. Barton Townley bought the property and 200 acres in 1944. He was knighted in 1960 and died, aged 76, at Lytham in June 1990.

Francis Charles Fahy and William Atkinson's

Another motoring pioneer was Francis Charles Fahy, who became a leading Councillor at Morecambe and the first Roman Catholic to be appointed to that borough's Bench.

Of Irish parents, he served his apprenticeship as an automobile engineer with William Atkinson and Sons, of Lancaster and Kendal. In 1913, he realised the potential of motor buses for passenger transport, and in conjunction with the Lancaster and District Tramways Company, was the first to run buses between Morecambe and Lancaster.

Atkinson's themselves were pioneers of the motor car industry in the Lancaster area. About 1903, backed by the experience of cycle and motorcycle manufacture, they started experiments in the building of a motor car at their Market Street premises.

This was the John O'Gaunt car, the first car to be made in Lancaster, all the parts being made by Atkinson's, and the engine supplied by a London company. The first car was assembled in about six weeks by Joseph Atkinson and his assistants. When it appeared on the streets of Lancaster, it was a sensation. The braking system was worked by a rope and it was something of a gamble as to whether the pulleys would work.

The John O'Gaunt car was not the first car to be seen on Lancaster's streets, although the honour did fall to a car brought in by Atkinson's. That vehicle was an International Mercedes Benz, made to look like a gun carriage and used in the celebrations for the Relief of Mafeking in 1900 in the Boer War.

However, to return to the John O'Gaunt car, Mr. Atkinson himself drove the first of the cars down a ramp over St. George's Hall, Liverpool steps for a very early motor show, and this resulted in enquiries about the car from all over the country.

Competition became keen, however, as the newfangled automobile trade took off, and Atkinson's retired from the car manufacturing market. The firm changed hands just after the First World War.

Eventually Joseph Atkinson retired to Morecambe, where he ended his days a happy man, secure in the knowledge that he had made a great contribution to local history and life.

Music Notables

J. A. Fuller-Maitland

Musicians have featured prominently in the history of the city. Near Lancaster lived one of the leading musical critics of his day, J. A. Fuller-Maitland, for 22 years music critic of The Times. He lived at Borwick Hall, one of the many stately old mansions in the Lancaster area.

He was one of the founders of the influential Morecambe Musical Festival, of which he was for several years, President.

John Greenall

A gifted musician and successful composer, but a shy and retiring man who shunned the limelight, was John Greenall, who died aged 84 after a lifetime in music.

John, member of an old Lancaster family, started his career as an apprentice with the famous London piano firm, Kirkmans, where he learnt the techniques of harpsichord and piano building. He came back to Lancaster to work for Tomlinson's (now Kenneth Gardner's) but eventually launched out on his own, and worked on his own account until his retirement, about 1955.

In 1920, he published the first of his settings of the ancient Chinese poets in the translation of Cranmer Byng, under the pen name of Hubert Hall, and many other songs from the Chinese followed. Some of his settings of the Irish poets were sung by Plunket Green.

Before the Second World War, Greenall became fascinated with the poems 'Lays of a Countryman', by Basil Sleigh, whose father at the time was Vicar of Silverdale. Some of Greenall's settings for these were published in 1937, under his own name. He died in 1959.

Kenneth Gardner

Kenneth Gardner was the man who probably did more than any other to make recorded and broadcast music, and radio and television sets available to the people of Lancaster.

Nowadays, his name still graces shops in the area. He started the business in Penny Street in 1921, and it is still going strong.

First items to be stocked were gramophones and records ('recordings'), but he then rode on the back of the rapidly expanding world of radio. There are Lancastrians still who remember going to Gardner's to get the crystal sets with their 'cat's whiskers', and later the two- or three-valve battery receivers, operated with numerous glass cells of H.T., and bulky L.T. accumulators.

In 1943, Gardner's acquired the old-established business of Tomlinson's, New Street. This followed the death, the previous year of C. R. Tomlinson, the son of the founder of the business, more than a century previously.

Literal links

Charles Dickens

One of history's greatest figures in literature had a liking for Lancaster. On several occasions, Charles Dickens stayed at the Royal King's Arms Hotel, probably for the last time in 1861, nine years before his death.

On this occasion, his friend Wilkie Collins, (author of 'The Moonstone'), was with him. Dickens loved to read from his own works aloud, and these so-called 'penny readings' were very popular. His mode of announcing his visit to Lancaster was:

'Mr. Charles Dickens sends his compli-

ments to the master of the King's Arms at Lancaster and begs to say that he wishes to bespeak for tomorrow (Saturday afternoon and night), to private sitting-room and two bed-rooms, also a comfortable dinner for two persons at half past five. Mr. Dickens will be accompanied by his friend, Mr. Wilkie Collins, and as Mr. Collins has unfortunately sprained his leg it will be of great convenience to him if his bed-room is as near the sitting-room as possible. For the same reason Mr. Dickens will be glad to find a fly awaiting them at the station. They purpose leaving here by the mid-day train at 12.38. – County Hotel, Carlisle, Friday, Eleventh September, 1857.'

The Royal King's Arms was at this time kept by Joseph Sly.

The 1857 visit by Dickens was an interesting one, for though he is regarded by most as one of our greatest novelists, he was also a leading social reformer, and some of that experience and inspiration came from Lancaster.

Dickens, accompanied by the Rev. F. B. Danby, Chaplain of the County Asylum (now the Moor Hospital), made a tour of inspection there and subsequently visited the Castle.

As a result they jointly wrote a series of articles for 'Household Words', which Dickens edited, in October 1857, entitled 'The Lazy Tour of Two Idle Apprentices'. They described their visits and gave a full description of the old King's Arms (built in 1625, it was rebuilt in 1879) and the Castle, with details of an execution a century before.

Of the King's Arms, it was mentioned that there was a custom to supply bride's cake to the customers after dinner. This reference to the hostelry led to Dickens becoming friendly with the Slys. From time to time correspondence passed between them, especially at Christmas, when presents of game were sent.

In 'The Lazy Tour of Two Idle Apprentices' we read:

'I have heard there is a good old Inn in Lancaster, established in a good old house; an Inn where they give you bride-cake every day after dinner,' said Thomas Idle. 'Let us eat bride-cake without being married, or of knowing any body in that ridiculous dilemma'. Mr. Goodchild, with a lover's sigh, assented. They departed from the station in a violent hurry (for which, it is unnecessary to observe, there was not the least occasion), and were delivered at the fine old house that night. Mr. Goodchild concedes Lancaster to be a pleasant place,

The Royal King's Arms – associations with Dickens

a place with a fine ancient fragment of a castle, a place of lovely walks, a place possessing staid old houses richly fitted with old Honduras mahogany ... The house was a genuine old house of very quaint description, teeming with old carvings, and beams, and panels, and having an excellent old staircase, cut off from it by a curious fence-work of old oak, or of the old Honduras mahogany wood. It was, and is, and will be for many a long year to come, a remarkably picturesque house'.

The second visit by Dickens to Lancaster was on September 11, 1861, when during the day several prominent Lancastrians called upon him, including the Mayor and Vicar. He gave selections from his works in the old Music Hall (now the Grand Theatre) in St. Leonardgate.

He brought his own stage equipment and it was reported that he was in a little alcove with scarlet curtains around him. He was accompanied on the platform by Miss Georgina Hogarth (sister-in-law), and three daughters, one of whom was Mrs. Perugini, wife of Charles Collins, a brother of Wilkie Collins. On the following day he gave a recital to the boys at Lancaster Royal Grammar School.

Laurence Binyon

Lancaster was the birthplace of the Poet Laureate Laurence Binyon, for ever remembered for his poem 'For the Fallen', intoned every year at Poppy Day services. He was born at No. 1, High Street, where there is a commemorative plaque, one of only a few in a city remarkably short of such plaques. Binyon was born on August 10, 1869, and died in 1943.

In 1983, the poet and art historian's home was turned into a block of showpiece flats. It had been an old end-terrace house behind the headquarters of British Telecom, was dismantled stone by stone and the material used for the new flats at the corner of High Street.

Artistic Connections

S. J. Lamorna Birch

An artist much identified with Lancaster, though he spent the greater part of his life in Cornwall, and whose paintings will be found in the Lancaster area, was S. J. Lamorna Birch. His story is inspiring.

Born at Egremont, Cheshire, in 1869, eldest of a family of ten, when he was 12, he became an office boy in Manchester. However, he devoted his leisure hours at even so young an age, to his two favourite activities – painting and fishing.

His health was not good, and when he was 16 he came to Halton where he worked in the local mill on industrial design. He painted a number of pictures there, and came to the notice of the industrialist Sir Thomas Storey. He was subsequently invited to exhibit at the Storey Institute Art Gallery, and some of those paintings were bought for inclusion in the permanent collection. Birch then left the area for Cornwall.

Up to this time he was plain Mr. Birch. He took the name 'Lamorna' from the beautiful valley in which he went to live, to distinguish himself from another artist, also named Birch, associated with Cornwall.

Lamorna Birch went on to become an Associate of the Royal Academy in 1926 and an RA in 1934. He was also a member of the Royal Society of Painters of Water Colours. Among a number of his works in oil and water colour which went into the Lancaster collection, was one of Brookhouse. This was one of his early major works, bought by Frank Storey and bequeathed by him to the city gallery.

Walter Bayes

Another artist was Walter Bayes, R.W.S., who was a lecturer at the Storey Institute and a figure regarded with great affection in the five years he spent at Lancaster. Notable is that this painter's association with the city did not start until he was 77, when he took up his appointment at the Storey Institute.

An intellectual painter, often the source of controversy, he was from 1918 to 1934 Head of the Westminster Art School and throughout his life was a well-known art critic.

In April 1944, his London home and studio were demolished in an air raid, he and his wife having a narrow escape. About the same time, Leonard Barton, Principal of the Institute, was in London, contacted Bayes and asked if he would be interested in coming to Lancaster. Bayes agreed and became head of the painting department.

He is remembered as a remarkable figure. In spite of his age, he used to hurry up the three flights of steps to the Institute two at a time, and worked always with his jacket off and his hat on. Once started on a painting, he would keep at work, regardless of meal times, until the light failed him.

He returned to London in July 1949, when he was 81, having made many friends in Lancaster, and died in 1956.

Harry Titley Morris

A notable photographer was Harry Titley Morris, who lived at Quernmore, a few miles out of the city, and became a prominent Lancaster businessman. He was equally well known for his photography, despite being an 'amateur'. The managing director of the floor coverings firm of Thomas Newall, Morris displayed his work, with outstanding success, in photographic exhibitions throughout the country, and in the United States. He was also an Associate of the Royal Photographic Society.

Morris had the distinction in 1947 of being created an Associate of the Photographic Society of America. This was at a time when there were only two other persons in Great Britain with Associateships. His photographs were published in many leading journals and periodicals. He died in late 1959.

Commercial Interests

Robert Gardner

The villages of the Lune Estuary, like Overton, Sunderland Point and Glasson, have fishing families going back for generations. One member of one of these families, Robert Gardner, who lived at the

Anchorage, Sunderland Point, became a leading Lancaster businessman.

Gardner was one of four sons and six daughters of Richard William Baxter Gardner, Harbour Master for the Port of Lancaster (Glasson Dock). Robert Gardner worked as a youth for J. H. Ball, shipbreakers, on St. George's Quay, Lancaster, later for Ball's successor, and eventually became owner of the business himself, his commercial empire growing to include quarries, property and warehouses.

William Marsland Pye

Despite its strong industrial history, Lancaster has a long agricultural tradition, and important among the old-established agricultural companies is Pye's, the corn and feedstuffs merchants.

The company was started by one of the grand old men of the city who lived to the ripe old age of 93, not dying until the late 1950s.

William Marsland Pye was born at Greenalls Farm, Quernmore. On leaving school in 1879, he became a warehouse boy in the old Fleet Square mill of James Bibby and Sons, of Conder Mill. He worked his way up through that firm, which in those days specialised in 'German patent flour'.

When J. Bibby and Sons, who were pioneers in the manufacture of compound cattle foods, transferred to Liverpool in 1886, Pye bought their Lancaster business, going into a six-year partnership with his brother, John.

About 1920, following huge expansion of his company, Pye went into partnership with his three sons – James, Thomas and Robert – and a dynasty was formed. Branches of the firm were established at Kirkby Lonsdale, Bentham, Garstang, Pilling, Beetham, Witherslack, Sedbergh and Lindale.

Old man Pye was a prominent figure throughout the farming community of North Lancashire, West Yorkshire and Westmorland, and was also a well-known staunch Methodist. Three other sons – William Marsland Pye, George Francis Pye and Richard Mason Pye – became directors of the Lancaster firm Pye Motors Ltd.

There were two other sons, John, who was drowned in the canal at Thurnham in 1902, and Isaac, killed on active service in France in 1916.

William Marsland Pye was married twice. When he died in 1957, apart from his sons, he left his widow, a daughter (Ruth), 13 grandchildren and 11 great-grandchildren – truly a family that has stamped its mark on the history of Lancaster.

8

Politics and Politicians

Socialism

Maurice Webb

Lancaster is somewhat reticent about celebrating the life of one of its most famous political sons, Maurice Webb. Older members of the community remember a great day in February, 1950, when Webb, who had worked his way up to become chairman of the Parliamentary Labour Party, stood on a platform at Lancaster's Ashton Hall and told an audience of more than 2,000 that he had come to his native town in memory of George Lansbury, the former Labour Leader, who died in 1940, *'to try and make some more Socialists.'*

This was an emotional occasion, for it had been at a meeting at the Ashton Hall 26 years previously, that Webb became a Socialist after listening to Lansbury's silver tongue.

In 1950, Webb became Minister of Food in succession to John Strachey, and a Privy Councillor, the first Lancaster man to become a Minister of the Crown.

Webb's story is quite a romance of Socialist polities. He was a shooting star almost from the word go.

He began his political work with the local Labour Party, and at the tender age of 22 was appointed full-time agent to Skipton Divisional Labour Party. Within three years he was given charge of a new Propaganda Department at Labour Party Head Office, thus entering mainstream politics, and he thrived.

He then became Political Correspondent of the old Labour Party paper, the Daily Herald, moving on to a similar position at the Daily Express. First elected to Parliament in 1945, he was, also at that time, appointed chairman of the Parliamentary Labour Party.

Maurice Webb was a stoical man. He never made much of the amputation of a leg after illness and continued to lead a very active life. When he died in 1956 there were many tributes, some from the great and good. Lord Attlee, who was Prime Minister when Webb was in the Government, commented,

> *'When he came into the House of Commons, it looked as if he would go far,*

and as chairman of the Parliamentary Labour Party during the early years of the Labour Government, he showed very high qualities. Then tragedy came. A serious illness resulted in the loss of a leg, and during the rest of his life he suffered severe pain.'

Herbert Morrison described Webb as a champion of the rights of MPs and an excellent Minister of Food, and Hugh Gaitskell, Leader of the Labour Party, said,

'The death of Maurice Webb is very sad news indeed. As agent, organiser, MP and Minister of the Crown, he devoted his life and considerable talents to the service of the Labour Party.'

As an aside on Webb, his youngest brother, Harold, was also a journalist. At one time, he was on the Lancaster Guardian, and he too went on to join the staff of the Daily Herald. A formidable family, the Webbs.

Bribery and Corruption

In the 18th and 19th centuries, the Lancaster Division was nationally notorious for the bribery and corruption seen openly at its elections.

Matters came to a head in 1865, when after the election of the two Liberal candidates, Edward Matthew Fenwick and Henry William Schneider, proceedings were started to unseat them, corrupt practices being alleged by the defeated Conservative, Edward Lawrence.

Commissioners began their sittings, which lasted five weeks, at the Shire Hall on July 26, 1866, heard sorry tales of scandalous behaviour, and Lancaster was disenfranchised the following year. Some voters received bribes from the Liberals and Conservatives and the going rate was about £8 a vote – big money in those days.

Lancaster was a hot-bed of Socialism around the turn of the century and indeed, it was the curious relationship between the Socialists and the mega-employer Lord Ashton, that eventually led to his virtual rejection of the city to which he had given so much (see Chapter Two).

The Suffragettes

Mary Ann Redhead

Among these Socialists were women who did their bit in the Suffragettes' struggles. One outstanding figure was Mary Ann Redhead, the daughter of a working-class family from Stirling Road.

As early as 1908, she took part in

famous marches through the streets of London, carrying a banner and wearing the Suffragettes' colours of purple, green and white. She became a familiar figure at demonstrations in the provinces and served prison terms in London, Yorkshire and East Lancaster.

Her part in local history is not well known, but she was a brave woman. When serving a two-month sentence in Holloway, she had to be taken to the Royal Free Hospital, such was the seriousness of internal injuries following being crushed against the railings of No. 10 Downing Street by a police horse.

Bitter Elections

The early years of the present century saw several bitterly-contested elections. Before the First World War, the Lancaster Division was mainly Liberal. However, this by with comparatively small majorities, the least being 44, by which Sir Norval Helme beat the sitting Conservative Member, Col. William Foster, of Hornby Castle, in 1900.

From that time to 1918, the Division was Liberal, but in that year a Coalition Unionist, General Sir Archibald Hunter, a distinguished soldier with local connections, overturned the Liberal, Sir Norval Helme.

Lord Ashton v Lloyd-George, 1928

There was a hard-hitting election in 1923, when J. J. O'Neill unseated the Conservative, John Singleton. He turned a 10,000 Conservative majority of the previous year into a 5,500 Liberal majority. In 1924, Sir Gerald Strickland, former Governor of Malta, mainly through the influence of Lord Ashton, defeated O'Neill by 3,431.

When Strickland was elevated to the peerage in 1928, there followed one of the most bitter by-elections ever in the Lancaster Division. There were three candidates: R. Parkinson Tomlinson, Liberal, a corn miller and Methodist local preacher, Herwald Ramsbotham, Conservative, and the Rev. D. R. Davies, Labour.

Just as today, the heavyweights of politics suddenly found great interest in areas of which they previously would have needed maps to even locate, and Lloyd George spoke for the Liberal Tomlinson at a huge and noisy meeting in the Winter Gardens at Morecambe.

The Liberals were confident of victory, but Lord Ashton shocked all by openly and with vinegar-tipped pen supporting the Conservative Ramsbotham. He made a direct attack on Lloyd George in a way that would make modern so-called hard-bitten politicians quail.

> 'The present position of the Liberal Party is entirely due to Mr. Lloyd George, and it is almost certain that it cannot recover from that position for a generation to come. You have said that Mr. Lloyd George is a dangerous man. Yes, he is more dangerous, in my opinion, than moderate members of the Labour Party.'

> 'I cannot forget how he has tried to make political capital out of grave national emergencies; how, for instance, at the time of the General Strike, he was disloyal to his party and his country, whilst his protest against the Defence Force being sent to Shanghai to save British lives from fiendish massacre and British women from the grossest insults and unspeakable barbarity, such as took place at Nanking, was a crime against humanity. Mr. Lloyd George may be able to sway emotional audiences, but I fervently trust that the electors of this division will not be deluded by his suspicious oratory.'

Lloyd George was furious and immediately dashed up from London to call Lord Ashton to account. Tomlinson won and, under the headline 'Hypnotized by the Wizard's Spell', the Morecambe Visitor commented

> 'Lloyd George's dramatic eve-of-poll visit hypnotized the electorate. They were swept off their feet. The Welsh Wizard had waved his wand, and the constituency succumbed to his spell ... In an outburst of emotionalism the Liberal was returned and the seat lost to Conservatism.'

Herwald Ramsbotham

Herwald Ramsbotham was a prominent figure who became Governor-General of Ceylon, now Sri Lanka. He represented the Lancaster Division as a Conservative from 1928 to 1941, and was later Parliamentary Secretary, president of the Board of Education, Minister of Pensions and First Commissioner of Works. He was raised to the peerage in 1941 as Lord Soulbury.

In 1944, he was appointed chairman of the Ceylon Commission, and in 1948 was at Colombo when the Duke of Gloucester read the King's Speech from the throne at the ceremony which marked the establishment of the Dominion of Ceylon. Lord Soulbury played a major role in drawing up the constitution of this. How sad he would be to see the state of the present Sri Lanka.

Sir Archibald Hunter

General Sir Archibald Hunter, Coalition Unionist MP for the Lancaster Division from December 1918 to November 1922, was a derring-do character. As his rank suggests, he had a distinguished military career, being Lord Kitchener's right-hand man in the Sudan, taking part in the defence of Ladysmith in the Boer War, and having the Aldershot Command from 1914 to 1917.

When he died in mid-1936, he was the oldest honorary surviving Freeman of Lancaster. A memorial to Sir Archibald Hunter, G.C.B., G.C.V.O., D.S.O, T.T., D.L. (gosh, what a lot of letters!) was unveiled in Lancaster Priory and Parish Church a year after his death, at the same time as the laying up of the Colours of the 2nd Batt. The King's Own Royal Regiment (Lancaster) in the church.

Hunter was a soldier of the old Imperial-colonial style, the stiff upper lip never quivering. It is easy to mock these days, but men like Hunter were fierce patriots, willing to die for their country and beliefs.

He joined the regiment in June 1874, and rose to national recognition as an heroic figure. He served in the Egyptian Army from 1884 to 1898, and for his services in the re-conquest of the Sudan, was promoted to Major-General at the early age of 39, receiving the thanks of both Houses of Parliament.

During the Boer War, Hunter was Chief of Staff to Sir George White, was Governor of Gibraltar from 1910 to 1913, and Colonel of the regiment from 1913 to 1926. He was made an Honorary Freeman of Lancaster in January 1899, and died in 1936, at the age of 79 years.

Sir Ian Fraser

A memorable politician of more recent years was Sir Ian Fraser, who was blind. Fraser, was first elected for the then Lonsdale (changed to the Morecambe and Lonsdale in 1950) Division in 1940, and played a prominent part in local and national politics.

He took a leading part in the British Legion (later Royal British Legion) and St. Dunstan's, the welfare organisation formed in 1915 for British Services Personnel. This led him to become known as the champion of ex-Servicemen.

The son of W. P. Fraser, of Johannesburg, Ian Fraser was educated at Marlborough and the Royal Military College, Sandhurst. He was a Captain in the Scottish Light Infantry in the First World War, and it was then, at the Somme in 1916 that he was blinded.

Fraser made nought of his blindness and was a wonderfully resolute man. After leaving hospital, he went to St. Dunstan's to take charge of the department dealing with after-care.

In 1921, he was made chairman of the organisation, a position he held for many years and which he made his life's work. In 1947, he became President of the British Legion, giving up the post in 1958 on being made a Life Peer.

Fraser had huge experience of life. He was a prominent member of the old London County Council for three years from 1922, but had always had Parliamentary ambitions. It therefore came as no surprise when in 1924, he was elected a Conservative MP for St. Pancras North. He was defeated in 1929 but re-elected in 1931 and 1935.

Fraser was knighted in 1934 and subsequently became a Companion of Honour. He was called to the Bar in 1931, and served two periods as a Governor of the BBC, 1937 to 1939 and 1941 to 1946.

With business interests in South Africa, he was a frequent visitor there. Regarded as a brilliant Parliamentarian, he was a regular and powerful speaker in the House, particularly on matters concerning ex-Servicemen.

In 1960, Lord Fraser of Lonsdale made history at the College of Heralds. The motto on his coat of arms – *Je Suis Pret* (I am ready) – was in Braille, the first time that any coat of arms had included Braille. It also contained the torch of St. Dunstan's, another symbol of his blindness.

9

Crime and Policemen

No. 2, Dalton Square

Council offices now occupy what was one of Lancaster's most notorious buildings, No. 2, Dalton Square. In the 1930s, this was the home of Dr. Buck Ruxton, who killed and mutilated his wife Isobel and maid, Mary Rogerson.

Ruxton, a Parsee-Indian, the city's first coloured doctor, dismembered the bodies and wrapped them in grisly parcels. He then drove to Scotland and threw the remains down a ravine near Moffatt, called, appropriately, the Devil's Beeftub.

He was caught after astute detective work by the English and Scottish police and several new forensic techniques were used in the case. Ruxton was hanged at Strangeways in 1936 after a sensational trial which attracted world-wide media interest.

The house in Dalton Square fell empty and semi-derelict for many years, unable to lose its macabre reputation. All uses of the premises seemed to come to nothing, and as recently as the 1970s, No. 2, Dalton Square had got into such a state that the local Council decided to take it themselves as offices. So where Ruxton calmly sliced up his wife and maid into small pieces, employees now pore over word processors and files.

Interest in the Ruxton case continues almost unabated. There are many who still remember the doctor, who was unlucky in that, at the time, Lancaster had an outstanding Chief Constable, H. J. Vann, who in 1937, went on to become Chief Constable of Maidstone, Kent. Proof of the popularity of the post at Lancaster was shown by there being 51 applications for the position when Henry Vann left Lancaster.

The Rogersons

The Rogerson family were particularly tragedy-struck. A sad echo of the Ruxton case came in February 1937, with the death at Lancaster Isolation Hospital (now the Beaumont College) in Slyne Road of 18-year-old Peter Rogerson, the brother of the maid, Mary.

Peter gave evidence against Ruxton at the trial, and it was actually he who first went to enquire about his sister at Ruxton's house when the girl was found to be missing. It must have been more than a poignant moment when Peter was buried in the same grave as his murdered sister at Overton churchyard.

Almost incredibly, tragedy nearly came into the lives of the Rogersons again in September 1937, when their nine-year-old son Robert was set on fire while playing. His life was saved by the prompt action of an employee of Morecambe Electricity Department. Robert Briggs, of Lancaster Road, Torrisholme, beat out the boy's burning clothing with a newspaper.

Robert had been playing near a bonfire on waste ground off Thornton Road, Morecambe, near his home, with his seven-year-old brother Walter and two other children. He caught fire when the

Dr Buck Ruxton and his wife Isobel

contents of a can of petrol or paraffin ignited.

The Ruxton Trial

Many expert witnesses in the Ruxton case wrote about it, such was its importance.

Professor James Couper Brash, Emeritus Professor of Anatomy at Edinburgh University, who collaborated with Professor John Glaister, of Glasgow, in preparing expert prosecution evidence, jointly published 'Medical-Legal Aspects of the Ruxton Case'.

Legal reputations were also made. John Singleton, the Judge, J. C. Jackson, who led for the Prosecution, Maxwell Fyfe, for the Crown, Norman Birkett, chief Defence Counsel, all went on to demonstrate brilliance.

Fyfe became Lord Chancellor and Home Secretary, was at the Nuremberg War Trials, and eventually became Lord Kilmuir; Birkett was also at the Nuremberg War Trials, and proceeded to the Lords, becoming Lord Birkett of Ulverston; and Singleton went on to become a Lord Justice of Appeal.

Other Executions
The Rawcliffe Case

Ruxton was hanged at Strangeways, but plenty of hangings took place at Lancaster itself. These took place behind the walls of the Castle, the last person to be hanged there being an unfortunate called Rawcliffe, who met his end on Tuesday, November 15, 1910. 31-year-old labourer, Thomas Rawcliffe, was found guilty of strangling his wife at their humble home, No. 1 Tyler's Yard, just off Cheapside.

It was a sordid case. Rawcliffe killed his 27-year-old wife while he was drunk. He had previously threatened to murder her, and at his trial little could be said in his defence, apart from that he had gone to the police himself and confessed. He was also known to have a history of behaving rather strangely and violently on occasions, since a fall from a three-storey high window in his youth. The defence claimed he was not of sound mind when he murdered Louisa Ann Rawcliffe.

Pathetically, when the police went to the house, they found a 15-month-old baby in bed next to its dead mother, and two other children, aged six and four years, asleep in a cot.

Thomas Rawcliffe gave himself up to PC Thomas Wilkinson, of the Lancaster Borough Police, and within four hours, at 10 am, was taken before the Borough Magistrates, when Wilkinson said Rawcliffe had shouted at him at 6.15 am,

> 'I have killed my wife. I strangled her last night at 7 o'clock. I must have been mad when I did it.'

The trial at Lancaster Assizes was a 'cut and dried' affair. The jury recommended mercy. The case became a cause celebre and there were huge crowds when Louisa Rawcliffe was buried. One local newspaper reported that

> 'special precautions were taken to prevent any untoward demonstration'

and that

> 'the people were very orderly throughout, and the funeral rites were of an impressive character.'

There was considerable public feeling about the case. Although at the trial, experts like the Superintendent of the Lancaster County Asylum (now the Moor Hospital) gave evidence that Rawcliffe was sane when he committed the killing – to which he pleaded Not Guilty – many members of the public disagreed, and a petition for his reprieve was organised.

The 1,500-signature petition was sent to the Home Secretary, the signatures including those of the Mayor and Town Clerk of Lancaster, prominent Lancaster townsmen and some medical staff at the County Asylum. The local MP, Norval W. Helme, also got involved. But it was all to no avail.

The morning of the execution was dank and chilly. The appointed hour was the traditional one of 8 am. Hundreds gathered outside the Castle walls. A few minutes before 8 am two warders mounted the top of the Castle Keep. At 8 o'clock precisely, there was a dull thud, the hand of one of the warders on the Keep was raised, and the bell of the Priory and Parish Church tolled, to confirm that Rawcliffe had been pitched into eternity.

It transpired that Rawcliffe had weighed 131 lb and that the hangman chose a drop of 8 ft. The condemned man had been 'perfectly composed' and went to the scaffold with a firm step. He made no request of any kind and gave no annoyance to the officials. He was no troublemaker in death.

James and Edith Henry Mills

Another notable case was that of James Henry Mills and his wife Edith. Not only did they commit a particularly brutal child killing, but Lancaster Castle also laid claim to an unsought record. It was here that for the first time for nearly 85 years a husband and wife were jointly sentenced to death in Britain.

The murder was one of the most callous the North West has seen, and there were few signs of sympathy when the Judge at Lancaster Assizes pronounced sentence of death:

'The sentence of the Court ... is that you will be taken from this place to a lawful prison and there taken to a place of execution and that you be hanged by the neck until you are dead ... and may the Lord have mercy on your souls.'

The year was 1935 and sentence was passed on the couple, both aged 62, of Blackburn, for the murder of Helen Chester, the three-year-old child of their next-door neighbours.

The trial was a two-day story of horror. The accused were an odd pair and the trial attracted tremendous notoriety. Neither showed much emotion when sentenced. The wife, stated to be very deaf, did not seem to comprehend what was going on.

For the Crown, the case was that little Helen disappeared one evening. Two months later, the charred body of the child was found with the arms and legs missing, the remains wrapped in a parcel in a yard next to the Mills' house.

Human bones which fitted the burnt body, buttons from the dead child's clothes, and a chain which she had been playing with, were found in the Mills' home, together with some blood-stained paper. The body was wrapped in half a quilt, (the other half of which was found on a bed in the Mills' house), and some pages of a newspaper missing from a copy of the paper in the Mills' house.

The whole of the case was something of an enigma. The Lancastrian lawyer J. C. Jackson, K.C., for the prosecution, admitted that he was unable to suggest a motive, but he commented that in recent times, many crimes had been committed for trivial motives.

During the hearing, a pathologist showed skulls to the jury to demonstrate how the child met her death with a hard blow, from behind, fracturing the skull and smashing into the brain. The jury also saw a blood-stained mallet found at the Mills' home. To this day, the case is one of mystery of motive. The death sentence on the couple was reprieved.

Chief Constables

William Thompson

One of several Chief Constables that Lancaster had until the Borough Force was absorbed into the County Force, was William Thompson, who took over from Henry Vann, who had made such a name for himself with the Ruxton case.

Thompson retired in 1947, on the day before the Borough Force, and his own office, ceased to exist. Two distinctions mark him out for special mention. Firstly, he was the only member of the Borough Police who rose to the rank of Chief Constable without having 'walked the beat' or worn a uniform. Secondly, he became chief of the force in which he started his career.

It was not surprising that Thompson was a shooting star, for he came from a police family.

Son of ex-Detective Inspector R. D. Thompson, he became a Detective Constable and Inspector of Weights and Measures (an area the police had charge of in those days), was promoted Detective Sergeant in 1925 and Detective Inspector in 1933). The following year he became Chief Constable of Clitheroe and returned to his native Lancaster in 1937 to succeed Vann.

This was not the complete story of the Thompson family's associations with the police, however. A brother, Chief Inspector R. Thompson, of the Rotherham Police, was appointed to the new post of Superintendent of the Rotherham Police.

Stanley Parr

More recently, a controversial Chief Constable of Lancashire, Stanley Parr, was sacked in December 1977 for malpractice, following a concerted campaign by the Preston-based Lancashire Evening Post. Parr served two spells of duty at Lancaster.

He returned to the city in 1957, where he had served for 15 months as Inspector in 1953-4 as Chief Inspector, to be second in charge of the Lancaster Division. On the second occasion, Parr came to Lancaster from the Lancashire Force Headquarters at Hutton, near Preston. Born at St. Helens, he joined the police in 1937.

During the Second World War, Parr was commissioned in the R.N.V.R. and was in the assault landing craft forces during the initial landings in Normandy, later seeing active service in the Far East on minesweeping operations.

A Rugby Football enthusiast, he formed the Lancashire Constabulary Rugby team. In 1962, at the age of 45, Parr became Chief Constable of Blackpool, going on to become Chief Constable of Lancashire in 1971. He died in 1985.

Lancaster's Prison

Lancaster today may not have its own police force, but it does have its own prison, in the Castle. In previous centuries, it earned a mixed reputation as a prison for debtors. It closed as a 'normal' prison in 1915, but was used for the internment of prisoners-of-war during the First World War. After the war, until 1937, it served as a training depot for recruits to the County Constabulary.

Its present use as a prison dates from 1955, when in April of that year, a party of 50 prisoners from Preston Jail were brought to Lancaster to continue their sentences, a total later building up to total about 300.

The first batch of prisoners occupied cells in the front portion of the Castle, near the massive John O'Gaunt entrance.

The previous October the Prison Commissioners had taken over part of the Castle for a five-year period. However, because they had to spend so much on the ancient property, they were granted a longer lease, and use as a prison will end by the turn of the century.

Luxury in Prison

In the days of the Castle as a debtor's prison, life was not quite as tough for some as might be imagined at first.

About 1840, there were between 300 and 400 debtors, where beer, wine and tobacco – but not spirits – were allowed to be brought in. Those whose friends came to the rescue could have any kind of food or clothing supplied. They also enjoyed the privilege of receiving visitors at more or less any time of day.

There were 'apartments' available to the debtors, furnished according to the generosity of their relatives and friends. It is recorded that the names of some of this accommodation were The Tap, The Snug, The Constable's, The Pin Box, The Smugglers, The Albion, The Belle Vue, The Strong Room and The Quakers.

But a lot of misery lay behind debt, and these men were not above organising themselves. In 1810, for instance, they petitioned Parliament in January:

'We, the Prisoners confined for debt, in his Majesty's gaol the Castle of Lancaster, beg leave thus publicly to address you, being the most part of us in prison generally through expenses (sic) incurred by costs, to the heavy calamity of us and our families; (We) humbly implore, that you will, the ensuing Meeting of Parliament, take our cause into your most serious consideration, and make such

alteration in the existing law, as to render them more uniform betwixt debtor and creditor.

The enormous expenses (sic) charged to recover small sums of money, are the ruination of both debtor and creditor; and many instances have occurred where both parties are confined in prison, to the great distress of numberless families, who are reduced to the greatest misery and want, while those confined are rendered useless members of the community, and no satisfaction obtained but revenge by those who confine them.'

Draconian Law

Life for some debtors may not have been so bad, but for some convicts, the laws of the day were draconian, the death sentence being applied to dozens of offences.

In 1794, for instance, Joseph Stonehouse and Joseph Garlick were sentenced to death for each stealing a horse, Thomas Parr for stealing a cow, and James Barlow for burglary and pocket-picking. Merry England indeed.

Chapel of St. Mary Magdalene

Behind the grey walls, prisoners nearly 40 years ago helped in the construction of one of the most modern prison chapels in the country – the Chapel of

St. Mary Magdalene.

It was transformed from an old chapel which had been disused and derelict since 1915. The chapel was dedicated by the Bishop of Lancaster, the Right Rev. A. L. E. Hoskyns-Abrahall, in 1958 at an impressive service attended by prisoners, members of the Prison Board and Board of Visitors.

In 1915, when the prison closed, the old chapel inside the Castle Keep was abandoned and a gallery and wooden pews removed. For the new chapel, the massive stone walls were smoothed and plastered and painted in delicate pastel shades. Pieces of scrap iron were turned into wall brackets for the lights, and a silver chalice brought back from Walton Jail, Liverpool, part of silver plate removed from Lancaster in 1915.

Tales of Sorrow

If the ancient stones of Lancaster Castle could weep, they would fill buckets. Who could fail to be moved by the letter written by a burglar serving 18 months in 1912 before he hanged himself? It was scrawled on a slate:

'To the Governor, I have made up my mind to chuck it. I have had it on my mind for some time. Now I'll do it.

Eighteen months with the companion I have is to (sic) much. I'd cure it with warm underclothing. I've asked long enough, God knows. 'A wasted life,' let me rot, as the gentleman said the other day (referring to a prison lecture). I'm sane enough now, but I shall not be if I have to wait 18 months here. Let my brother know, he had been insured, I believe. Good luck to you, may you live long to dish out bread and water to poor unfortunate devils in this benighted hole. Now I'll tell you why I've done it. First, people say there is a God. I am going to see. Second, toothache all along and no sleep at night. God! I'll cure that, though. Third, insufficient food, porridge like water, so is the soup. Well, that's enough. I'll go and burn in hell –

"Earth up, here lies an imp of hell
Planted by Satan's double.
Poor silly wretch, he's damn'd himself,
To save the Lord the trouble."

People will say I'm mad. Yes, perhaps so, in a sense. I've read about murderers eating their breakfast before being hung, so I ate my dinner. It was grand, though watery.'

Lancaster Castle floodlit at night

H.M. PRISON LANCASTER
WARNING

Under the Prison Act 1952 it is an offence for any person –

I. to help a prisoner to escape or attempt to escape: the maximum penalty is 5 years imprisonment (section 39 as amended by the Criminal Justice Act 1961);

II. without authority to convey or attempt to convey into a prison or to a prisoner intoxicating liquor or tobacco: the maximum penalty is six months imprisonment or a £50 fine or both (section 40);

III. without authority to convey or attempt to convey into or out of a prison or to a prisoner any letter or other article or to place it outside the prison intending it to come into a prisoner's possession: the maximum penalty is a £50 fine. (section 41)

A salutory reminder of Lancaster Castle's use as a prison

10

A City and its Landmarks

City Status

Lancaster was raised to the dignity of a city in Coronation year, 1937. The great day was in May, but before then, much behind-the-scenes lobbying had been carried out.

The start can be traced to a suggestion in November 1936, by Alderman E. C. Parr, chairman of the Finance Committee, at the Council's Annual Meeting. He said it would be particularly fitting as the Sovereign carried the title Duke of Lancaster.

The move then started in earnest, one report commenting on Lancaster's 'importance as a centre, its distinctive character, its progress in local government, its civic spirit and enthusiasm, the fact that it is the County town, the part it has played in history, its industrial activities, and the many-sided nature of its interests!

The lobbyists on Lancaster's behalf pointed out:

'There is no town more justified in this Coronation year to be created a city, and although its population cannot compare with the large cities of Manchester, Liverpool, Leeds, etc., its importance as the County town of that large and important County of Lancashire, its historical and Royal connections, its traditions and its distinct character, cannot be lightly overlooked. It is suggested that it would be particularly fitting for his Majesty as Duke of Lancaster to grant the title and dignity of a city by Letters Patent without a Lord Mayor and so give Lancaster the status which many County towns of similar size but of less importance now enjoy.'

The negotiations were carried out with great secrecy, even some members of the Council knowing little of them. In addition to Parr, a power behind the movement was Lancaster's Town Clerk, R. M. Middleton. He gave many years of dedicated service to Lancaster and must have been a very relieved man when the official announcement came through that Letters Patent were about to pass the Great Seal.

There was one slight disappointment for the people of the city. A statement was issued that,

'The Secretary of State desires to make it clear that the grant to the Borough of the status of a City does not in itself confer upon the Mayor the title of "Lord Mayor". The grant of this privilege is an entirely separate matter.'

Nevertheless, the Mayor immediately sent a telegram to the King making clear just how pleased Lancaster was:

'On behalf of the Mayor, aldermen and citizens of the ancient county town of Lancaster which your Majesty has been graciously pleased to raise to the title and dignity of a city on your Coronation Day, and for which I return the grateful and sincere thanks of your Majesty's loyal subjects in Lancaster for the great honour, I desire to convey respectful and sincere congratulations on the Coronation of your Majesties and desire to assure your Majesties of our affection and steadfast allegiance to the Crown. May your Majesties' reign be long, peaceful and prosperous.'

Regal links

Not the least reason for Lancaster's city ambitions was its long association with Royalty. The reigning monarch is the Duke of Lancaster. Queen Victoria was not *unamused* when, in the memorable year 1887, she found that a Jubilee medal struck in Lancaster had her as 'Duke of Lancaster'.

That was the year the industrialist Sir Thomas Storey received his knighthood, and announced his intention to provide Lancaster with an Institute. He went to Scotland taking with him a solid gold example of Lancaster's Jubilee medal with the 'Duke of Lancaster inscription.

Victoria was right royally pleased, George V endorsed the act of his grandmother, and today Queen Elizabeth II continues the tradition as Duke of Lancaster.

No special medal was struck to mark Lancaster becoming a city, but at celebrations in 1987 marking the 50th anniversary, a limited edition of 1,000 medals were produced. If you were fortunate enough to have got hold of one, you have a collector's item.

Lancaster may not have a 'Lord Mayor' but it does have all the necessary ingredients of a city. The Castle is one of the most notable in the country, it has its cathedral in the Roman Catholic St. Peter's, and the founding of Lancaster University in the 1960s has brought much prestige to the city and, like all cities, Lancaster seems always to be going through change.

'The Tourist Prison'

A good case in point is the Castle's use as a prison, soon to come to an end, when the complex will become a leading tourist attraction.

At present, tourists can visit only parts of the Castle, and it is well worth making the effort, but the hitherto 'secret' parts, known only to the prison staff and their 'guests,' will be fascinating when they become public.

There is talk of having the country's first national museum of law at the Castle. Certainly an appropriate location, as even in recent years it has been the scene of some of the country's biggest trials, that of the 'Birmingham Bombers' included. Of course, in 1991, the convictions of those men were found to be unsustainable and they were freed.

The courts here have heard of violence and death for centuries. The world turns, but little changes. In the 18th century, more prisoners were sentenced to death at Lancaster than at any other Assizes, and many hundreds were transported to Australia. However, there are some pleasant aspects of the Castle.

Pageantry

Every year, the Shield Hanging is held in the Shire Hall. The High Sheriff of Lancashire presents his shield to be hung alongside scores of others from down the centuries. In an age from which much colour and pageantry has disappeared, it is a reminder of yesteryear when such things were considered important.

Each High Sheriff's shield has an individual coat of arms portraying significant characteristics of his profession or interests. The shield is hung to the accompaniment of trumpet fanfares, with officials in the costumes of hundreds of years ago.

Change is hastening the old city towards the 21st century. The 1970s saw a reawakening by Lancaster of the value of its architectural treasures, such as the restoration of the Music Room by the Landmark Trust.

Sometimes change has been inflicted through fire. In 1983, a huge blaze gutted the King's Arcade, but its splendid facade was rebuilt. In 1984, the Market Hall went up in flames, but that has also risen again, Phoenix-like.

Above: Shire Hall

Left: Shire Hall Interior

Places of Interest

Ashton Memorial and Williamson Park

The Ashton Memorial was a gift of Lord Ashton, who started life as plain James Williamson. (Details of his life are given in Chapter Two). It stands in the park given by Lord Ashton's father, also called James, and dates from 1909.

Locally it is termed merely 'the Structure', or, irreverently, 'the Jelly Mould', and until the 1980s, it served no practical purpose at all. Having by then fallen into a state of near dereliction, a massive renovation scheme was undertaken.

Today, the Ashton Memorial has a multi-screen presentation on the Edwardians and Lord Ashton, and the ornate former Palm House beside it is now an exotic Butterfly House.

Assembly Rooms

A gem of 18th century architecture in King Street, but often overlooked by the hasty visitor to Lancaster.

In its hey-day, it was one of Lancaster's main venues and was built by the trustees of Alderman William Penny, whose Almshouses, or Hospital, is next door. Via a diminutive staircase, there is a splendid Music Room.

The Assembly Rooms has a variety of uses, including the holding of antiques and bric-a-brac sales.

The building had fallen into disrepair by 1987, but was restored to at least something approaching its former glory as Lancaster got to grips with its treasures of the past, at a time when other buildings were tumbling in redevelopment schemes.

The Canal

At one time, the 18th century canal linked Preston and Kendal, via Lancaster, with a 'branch' from Galgate to Glasson Dock. The Northern reaches, from Tewitfield to Kendal, are no longer navigable.

One of the major structures is the Aqueduct, opened in 1797, which carries the canal over the Lune. In addition to its beauty, the Aqueduct is statistically impressive. The five semi-circular arches are each of 70 ft span, the Aqueduct is 664 ft long and 53 ft high, and it all cost about £48,000. J. Y. W. Turner was so impressed that he painted a picture of it.

Carlisle Bridge

Carrying the main railway from London to Scotland over the Lune, just North of the Castle railway station, the bridge was reconstructed in 1962.

The first bridge was built in 1846 as a timber arch and replaced by a more substantial structure about 20 years later. It said much for the 19th century engineers that during the 1962 reconstruction, the stone piers were found to be in a good state of preservation, and were retained in the new bridge.

The Castle

Dating to the early years of the 13th century, the castle was built on the site of successive Roman forts. Owned by the Sovereign since 1399, and claimed to be the oldest working castle in the world, it has watched centuries of history pass, a great beacon blazing from its top at the time of the Spanish Armada.

The Castle is probably best known for having been the place of imprisonment of the Lancashire Witches in 1612. Most of the huge complex is today used as a prison, but various parts are open to the public, including the Shire Hall, Crown Court, dungeons, Hadrian's Tower and the Drop Room.

It was at the Castle that the last public execution took place in Lancaster in 1865. About 6,000 people from all over the county 'celebrated' the occasion by setting up fun fairs, side shows and various other jollities around the walls.

The Shire Hall dates to the 18th century. The former Assizes were held here, but were opened for the last time in 1971, when under reform of the law courts, Lancaster was stripped of its Assizes and Quarter Sessions.

This was despite great opposition from organisations including the Corporation, and the Lancaster, Morecambe and District Law Society. There is evidence of Assizes being held at the very start of the 13th century.

Castle Hill was formerly close-packed with terraced properties of all kinds, from humble artisans' cottages to warehouses. Much of it was cleared away in the late 19th century and in the early years of the present century, but the area on a dark and rainy night can still give the feel of what Lancaster used to be like. No. 15, Castle Hill is a museum which depicts an artisan's house of the era just before Victoria.

Duke's Theatre

A highly regarded theatre occupying the former St. Anne's Church, and one of the most imaginative uses of a redundant church in the North West. "The Duke's" has achieved a reputation in recent years for acclaimed outdoor productions in Williamson Park. Plans for the acquisition of the old St. Anne's Church for its use as a theatre were passed by Lancaster City Council in 1969.

In 1976, the theatre's art gallery was named the Housman Gallery after the first Minister of St. Anne's. To mark this, a portrait of the Rev. Housman was permanently loaned by Mr. Housman Symons, the late vicar's last surviving direct descendant.

A leading light in the founding of the Duke was Charles Haggith, who died in 1989, aged 64. He was so enthusiastic that he walked the streets of the city to knock on doors and drum up interest.

Friend's Meeting House

Lancaster has a strong Quaker tradition. George Fox himself, the founder of the Society, was imprisoned in the Castle in 1664. The Friends' Meeting House was originally built in 1677, though the present building is of later date.

The Quakers became a force to be reckoned with throughout the whole of this part of Lancashire.

The Friends' Meeting House, in Meeting House Lane

There was formerly a Friends' School in Lancaster, the George Fox School, but that closed in the mid-1980s amidst much public regret. Fox came to Lancaster for the first time in 1652 and preached there on several occasions, causing turbulent scenes.

Grand Theatre

An example of how theatre can be kept alive if only there are enough enthusiasts. The Grand dates to 1782, opening on the evening of Monday, June 10.

It went through a chequered career, and at least two changes of name until 1908, when its interior was gutted by fire. The fire is said to have started when an actor placed his hat over a gas lamp. The original walls still stood, however, and the theatre re-opened seven months later as 'The Grand,' previous names having been 'The Athenaeum' and the 'Music Hall'.

Its future was in jeopardy in 1930, when its owners went into liquidation, but it was taken over by a cinema company. However, despite some theatrical activity in the 1940s, the building was for sale in 1950.

The Grand's saviour was the Lancaster Footlights Club, who bought it. They had put on plays there previously, and have continued to the present day.

The Grand is one of the oldest theatres in the country still operating in its original building. Only the Theatre Royal at Bristol and York having been in continuous use for a longer period. The Grand came near to demolition in the 1950s, during redevelopment of the area around St. Leonardgate.

The Guardian

One of the longest-established weekly newspapers in the country, having been first published on Saturday, January 28, 1837. Its various editions stretch into Yorkshire.

The paper is published by Lancaster and Morecambe Newspapers Ltd., who also publish sister paper, The Morecambe Visitor, which is of a little more recent origin, dating to 1874.

Horse Shoe Corner

One of the best-known points in Lancaster. Legend has it that John O'Gaunt's horse cast a shoe here, but in reality, the horse shoe set in the ground marks the holding of horse fairs on the site.

Judges' Lodging

Particularly prominent at the head of Church Street, dating to the 1620s and built as the private residence of one Thomas Covell, six times Mayor of Lancaster and Keeper of the Castle for nearly half a century.

It gets its name from the Lancaster Assizes, when the Judges stayed here. It now houses two museums, one devoted chiefly to furniture of the Gillow company, the other a Museum of Childhood. The Cross in front of the Lodgings was put up originally to the memory of Covell, who died in 1639.

Kingsway

The Baths were first opened in 1939 and completely renovated and updated into a modern leisure centre in 1983. Kingsway, the road, was built by First World War prisoners.

Moor Hospital

Started life in 1816 as the huge 'County Lunatic Asylum', with about 80 acres of grounds and occupying the site of a

The Judge's Lodgings

former racecourse. It has been an important employer in Lancaster and formerly had thousands of patients.

In recent years, the hospital has been reduced in size, and is expected to close within the next few years.

Museum (City)

This is situated in Market Square, in the old Town Hall that served Lancaster until Lord Ashton gave the new Town Hall in Dalton Square in 1909.

You'll find everything about Lancaster's past here in a museum which has a considerable reputation for its innovative displays and exhibitions.

Here also is the Museum of the King's Own Royal Regiment. The regiment dated to 1680 and was headquartered at

Lancaster in 1880 at Bowerham Barracks, now St. Martin's College. The King's Own Royal Regiment was amalgamated in the late 1950s with the Border Regiment to form the King's Own Royal Border Regiment.

Museum (Maritime)

Housed in the old Custom House of Richard Gillow, dating to 1764, this is an outstanding building on St. George's Quay.

'The Maritime Museum' explores not only the maritime and canal history of Lancaster, but also its present and future, with displays about the Morecambe Gas Field. Look out for the 'Sir William Priestley', the former Morecambe fishermen's lifeboat and other craft.

The Maritime Museum was formally opened in 1985 by Lord Montagu of Beaulieu. In 1988, it was one of only 12 winners in the country of a British Tourist Authority 'Come to Britain' award.

Music Room

Tucked away up the alleyway into Sun Street, this Italianate building dates to the 18th century and was built originally as a pavilion.

Until the mid-1970s, the ornate Music Room was hemmed in by 'grotty' buildings of various kinds, including a builder's yard. Rescue came in the form of the Landmark Trust.

In the Music Room, look out particularly for the plasterwork, which, representing the nine Muses and 12 Roman

The old Custom House, now the Maritime Museum

Reflections on Lancaster

Emperors, is thought to be the work of a famous Italian stuccadore, Vassali. The area in which the Music Room stands was once the garden of the Rev. Dr. Oliver Marton, Vicar of Lancaster from 1767 to 1794.

In 1967, a plan was mooted for the building to be moved stone by stone to a new site but nothing came of it. The restored Music Room was opened by the Queen in 1977, during her Silver Jubilee tour of Lancashire.

The Music Room (above) and , right, an example of the mouldings to be seen

Nuffield Hospital

Situated at Meadowside, the Lancaster and Lakeland Nuffield Hospital, in a striking modern building, opened in 1985 as the city's first private hospital. The building was previously Storey's research laboratories.

Penny's Hospital

In King Street, and dating to the will of William Penny, 1715. In the 1960s, Penny's Hospital was sold by the Trustees to Lancaster Corporation and in 1969, the new William Penny's flats in Regent Street were built.

Priory and Parish Church

Dedicated to St. Mary and the successor to an 11th century Priory of Benedictine, little of what you see predates the 14th century, and the tower was rebuilt in 1755.

Of particular interest are the intricately carved choirstalls, and the King's Own Memorial Chapel. There are many fine memorials both inside and outside the church, including one of a reclining woman who, unfortunately, in December 1991, was 'beheaded' by vandals. An unpleasant sign of the times.

Ripley School

Ripley St. Thomas' Church of England School, an Aided Secondary School provided by Church of England Trustees, is known for its outstanding buildings, which date to 1864. The school was founded and endowed by Julia Ripley, widow of a Lancaster-born Liverpool merchant.

Originally Ripley's was for Lancaster and Liverpool children. The school has a museum and a beautiful chapel. The present set-up at the school dates to

The memorial at Lancaster Priory and Parish Church – prior to beheading by vandals

1966, with the merging of Ripley Boys' C.E. and St. Thomas' C.E. Schools.

Mr. George Phythian, appointed headmaster when Ripley opened as the amalgamated school, retired in 1991, after a notable headship.

Rocking Horse Sign

A rare survivor of the signs that were once commonplace over shops. The Rocking Horse over Lawson's toy shop in New Street marks one of the old-established businesses of the city.

It was in 1855 that Mr. and Mrs. B. R. Lawson started a toy shop in church Street, later moving to Penny Street. In 1933, came the move to New Street, the Rocking Horse sign moving with them, now one of the best-known symbols in Lancaster.

Royal Albert Hospital

An important psychiatric hospital which dates to 1868, and when opened first served the whole of the North of England. It was designed by local architect E. G. Paley, and cost the then huge sum of £204,300. At one time, the Royal Albert Hospital and its grounds covered more than 200 acres.

As with the Moor Hospital, the Royal Albert has been substantially reduced. The hospital has some bizarre reminders of the past, including a barrel in which a deformed boy lived until being admitted to the Royal Albert about 1910.

An old engraving of Ripley School

Royal Grammar School

One of the oldest schools in the country, it can trace its history to 1235. Many of the old buildings you see today in East Road are of the 19th century. A considerable number of famous men have been educated here.

Queen Victoria was a good friend to the school and it was through her it was given the accolade, 'Royal'. In 1851, she directed that £100 be paid from the Duchy of Lancaster revenues towards the restoration of the school, and permitted it to take the name 'Royal'.

Lord Ashton was also a benefactor, but he had been a pupil demonstrating mixed abilities. In exams in 1854, he was near the bottom of the form in Latin and Arithmetic, but top in History and Geography. The politician, Cecil Parkinson is a former pupil of the School.

Part of Lancaster Royal Grammar School

Royal Lancaster Infirmary

Dates to 1896, and today has a catchment area of patients from Kendal in Cumbria, to several miles south of Lancaster. The hospital has seen great expansion over recent years, the old buildings being entirely dwarfed by shiny new ones. In 1990, a £21 million extension scheme was approved.

St. George's Quay

Until the late 18th century sailing ships, many of them trading with the West Indies, sailed up the Lune to here in the heart of Lancaster. Later Glasson Dock became the Port of Lancaster.

Among major cargoes landed at St. George's Quay were mahogany, rum, sugar, cotton and tobacco. Much of the mahogany would have been used by the Gillow furniture-making company.

St. John's Church

One of Lancaster's outstanding churches but, ironically, redundant. Best known for its tower, the church was known for many years as the 'Corporation Church', because it was so closely associated with the Corporation. Dating from 1755, it is now looked after by the Redundant Churches Fund, and is used occasionally on special occasions.

St. Martin's College

Founded by the Church of England in 1963, in the old Bowerham Barracks of the King's Own. The 19th century castle-like building now has some interesting modern architecture around it.

St. Martin's has over 1,000 full-time students taking first degree, postgraduate and teachers' in-service courses.

St. Peter's R.C. Cathedral

One of the finest churches in the city and a landmark because of its impressive, soaring spire.

Built in 1859 to the designs of local architect E.G. Paley, architect of churches throughout the area, it was raised to Cathedral status in 1925.

Sainsbury's

It is not usual for a book to mention individual commercial enterprises, but in the case of Sainsbury's at Lancaster it is entirely justified, it being one of the most harmonious developments in the city for many years.

Fronting on to Cable Street, the store retains the original stone frontage of Lancaster's first baths, given to the town by MP Samuel Gregson in 1863.

The Storey Institute

Skerton Bridge

Every visitor to Lancaster will go through the 'Skerton Bridge experience'. Despite the building of the Lancaster by-pass in the Sixties, the M6 and various other roads, the flow of traffic over poor old Skerton Bridge is incessant (and sometimes very slow indeed). The bridge dates to about 1788.

Storey Institute

Presented to Lancaster by industrialist Thomas Storey, this was erected to celebrate the Golden Jubilee of Queen Victoria. It was extended some years later by his son, Herbert Lushington Storey.

For many years its chief use was as an Art College and Art Gallery, but its future use is uncertain. Lancaster University has made overtures about acquiring the building.

The Storey Institute carries on a long tradition of education on the site, for there was formerly here a Mechanics' Institute.

The Town Hall

An imposing building in Dalton Square given to Lancaster by Lord Ashton and opened in December 1909. It was designed by E. W. Mountford and is constructed of Longridge stone.

It replaced a less grand Town Hall in Market Square, now the City Museum. Mountford was often called 'Town Hall Mountford' for his speciality in designing municipal buildings. He died before Lancaster's was completed.

The University

Dates to 1964, when the first students arrived to St. Leonard's House in the city. The occupancy of the Bailrigg site, a mile or two out of Lancaster, took place two years later. The University has now grown to become recognised as one of the best.

In 1990, a collection of paintings and historical documents which had belonged to John Ruskin was brought here.

In 1991, it was decided that the University was a fitting place as the home of one of the most important collections of legal manuscripts in Europe, compiled by the Record Commission of Great Britain – 1,680 volumes of texts and calendars dating from the 12th century. There is also an important Wordsworth collection.

In recent years the University has seen great expansion, including the building of an £8 million hotel complex, opened in 1991.

Victoria Statue

Another of Lord Ashton's many gifts to Lancaster, at around the same period as the Town Hall. Below the massive figure of Queen Victoria are 'friezes' of the leading men and women of science, art and literature of the times, all conveniently named.

Westfield War Memorial Village

A near-unique war memorial opened in October 1924, by Earl Haig. The idea for the village was first mooted by the eminent local landscape architect T. H. Mawson, who advocated a village settlement in his book, 'An Imperial Obligation'. The scheme was made possible by the magnificent gift of the site by the family of Sir Thomas Storey.

The village started with 13 houses, occupied by disabled men and their families. The foundation stone of the first two cottages was laid in November 1919, by Lord Richard Cavendish.

White Cross

Opposite the Royal Lancaster Infirmary, and now the home of many commercial and industrial units, the former White Cross Mills was the main premises of Storey Bros. and Co., one of the biggest employers in the city.

That use came to an end during a period when many of Lancaster's large factories were closing. The site was then acquired by Lancashire Enterprises Ltd. One of the sights here used to be a 250 ft. high brick chimney. It collapsed in 1966, killing two people. Miraculously, the chimney fell between buildings and not on them, otherwise the death toll would have been much higher.